THE NORMAL ALCOHOLIC

THE NORMAL ALCOHOLIC

William F. Kraft, PhD

ALBA·HOUSE  NEW·YORK

SOCIETY OF ST. PAUL, 2187 VICTORY BLVD., STATEN ISLAND, NEW YORK 10314

ST PAULS

Library of Congress Cataloging-in-Publication Data

Kraft, William F., 1938-
 The normal alcoholic / William F. Kraft.
  p.   cm.
 Includes bibliographical references.
 ISBN 0-8189-0853-X
 1. Alcoholics — Mental health.   2. Alcoholism — Physiological
aspects.   3. Self-management (Psychology)   4. Alcoholism.
I. Title
RC565.K66   1999
616.86'1 — dc21   99-13953
                                                CIP

Produced and designed in the United States of America by the
Fathers and Brothers of the Society of St. Paul,
2187 Victory Boulevard, Staten Island, New York 10314,
as part of their communications apostolate.

ISBN: 0-8189-0853-X

Printing Information:

Current Printing - first digit   1   2   3   4   5   6   7   8   9   10

Year of Current Printing - first year shown

1999   2000   2001   2002   2003   2004   2005   2006   2007

In Gratitude to

POTADA,
A.A., Al-Anon,
Alcoholic, Co-Alcoholic, and
Non-Alcoholic Friends

Preface

One can question the validity of a book on "the normal alcoholic" and on "normal modes of alcoholism" arguing that because alcoholism is a disease or at least a disorder, alcoholics and alcoholism cannot be normal. And yet, contrary to popular belief, alcoholics often have a good job, money, and reputation as well as being good persons. Furthermore, many alcoholics are far from daily drinkers, and others drink with control. They are more like "us" rather than "them." So, is it possible to be normal and alcoholic — or, is "normal alcoholism" an oxymoron?

Many journeys with alcoholics as well as considerable research on alcoholism have convinced me that it is not only possible but actually likely for most alcoholics to be normal. While it is true that some alcoholics behave abnormally and manifest symptoms of a primary disease (and for them, the effects of drinking are devastating), still, most alcoholics are more normal than abnormal insofar as they satisfy needs, are successful and responsible, adhere to social norms, circumvent legal trouble, and avoid abnormality. But they are alcoholics nonetheless insofar as they are obsessed with and compelled to drink alcohol that results in more negative than positive consequences.

These so-called normal alcoholics are sometimes called "functional alcoholics," that is, they function relatively well (are normal), and they drink alcoholically. Even though they do not manifest blatant symptoms, they are nevertheless in alcoholic trouble. A problem and challenge, however, lies in the fact that, in contrast to more dysfunctional/abnormal alcoholisms, little has been written about the meaning and treatment of more functional/normal alcoholisms.

If alcoholism can be normal, then what is alcoholism? What is normality? What is normal alcoholism? How is it similar to and different from abnormal alcoholism? Can it lead to more debilitating forms of alcoholism? How does it impact on self and others? Why are normal modes of alcoholism seldom treated? What are the consequences of such denial and avoidance? How can you help yourself and others recover from the more ordinary forms of alcoholism? Or, why recover if you are normal? This book is a response to such questions.

There are many kinds of alcoholics, and they react differently to alcohol. Some are verbal and funny, while others are quiet and serious. Some are kind and gentle, while others are mean and rough. Some are responsible and dependable, and others are not. Some alcoholics can drink heavily and still act normally, while others drink relatively little and undergo acute personality changes. My agenda is to develop a model of alcoholism that includes various ways to be alcoholic. The proposed paradigm incorporates the vision of Alcoholics Anonymous as well as other ways to construe alcoholism. My hope is that this book will help us recognize and respond compassionately and competently to all alcoholics.

I am grateful to many people. Among these providers, I thank patients and students as well as alcoholic, co-alcoholic, and sober friends, especially Chuck G., Libby S., Rex P., and Sharon and Ron G. for their suggestions, support, and help. Gratitude is also offered to Pat Frauenholz and Janine Geibel for their patient and competent typing. Finally, I thank my family and God for their presence.

Table of Contents

I Her and His Stories

Stories speak to the heart, theories to the mind. Sharing and listening to our hearts and minds can help us to look, think, choose, act, and feel better. We will look at alcoholism from both of these perspectives — from personal, affective, and spontaneous stories and from more impersonal, cognitive, and systematic theories. Let us begin by listening to a couple of stories.

Her Story

"My name is Mary, and I'm an alcoholic. My alcoholism may not fit your view of alcoholism, that is: of being irresponsible and out of control. Actually, I managed well, seemingly as well as and often better than my peers. Really, I was successful, articulate, enjoyable, helpful, responsible, accountable, you name it — I had it. But beware, I was also and am alcoholic. My story is not so dynamic and exciting that it evokes awe, but rather it is more mundane and normal.

"I had my first drink when I was about five years old. I can recall sipping some of my dad's beer, and everyone thinking it was cute. I know now that my dad along with most of the men and women in our extended family were alcoholics. It was simply normal to drink alcoholically.

"Speaking of my dad, he was an amazing and lovable alco-

1

holic. He would drink only on his days off, which was once a week at best. And he never drank conspicuously or to the extent of being drunk. Anyhow, my dad never missed work, rarely got angry, was usually mild and quiet, and was always busy. You can say, I became a chip off the old block.

"Another 'old block' of which I am a 'chip' is my mother. What can I say about my mother? Unlike my dad, she rarely drank, and then just one drink. I guess my mother was the classic co-alcoholic — a person who denied, tolerated, took responsibility for, and enabled my father's alcoholic behavior. She was and is a good woman of the old school. Her primary purpose in life was to serve and make others happy. That's my mother: a loving and lovable poor soul.

"Anyhow, like most kids my development was influenced by both mom and dad. I became a faithful and dedicated wife and mother who served others to a fault. And like my father, I became an alcoholic teacher who succeeded professionally. I am a co-dependent, an adult child of an alcoholic family, and an alcoholic. Actually, it's not as bad as it may sound; in fact, life was good, and it got better when I got sober.

"To jump ahead, when I was 25 years old I got married, and we had three children. Since mothering was paramount to me, I quit teaching and only drank at festive occasions. I was a model mother. After my youngest was in school, I became a workaholic and an active alcoholic.

"During the week, I would start work at seven and return home around the same time as my kids. One of my rules was that I never drank during the week before my kids were in bed. But when everyone was in bed, I would have several drinks, read the paper, mellow out, and fall asleep. Later, I would awaken and go to bed. Overtly, I didn't cause much harm. But as they say, I was often 'out to lunch' especially with my husband. Try to share with someone who is in her own world. Try to talk to or play with someone who is passed out.

"On weekends, I would step on my drinking accelerator and

drink in the afternoons. While I became pleasantly buzzed, I did chores around the house and even drove the kids to various lessons and events. Good grief, the chances I was taking! I know that God was with me, for I never had an accident or even got a ticket. I sure could have. Anyhow, on Sunday after church and brunch, I would have two strong drinks and then begin sobering up to prepare myself for the work week.

"I was mainly a polished, closet drinker. Though I drank alcoholically, in public I was as normal as anyone, and nobody called me an alcoholic. In fact, relatives saw me as the sober one. At conventions, I would never drink while networking and attending workshops. But when the day was over and I returned to my hotel room, I would polish off a pint, become pleasantly buzzed, and go to sleep.

"In my early forties, my dad and a friend died. During my dad's funeral I had very little to drink, but a few weeks later I began to drink more. I still functioned well, but with more hangovers, fatigue, and more preoccupation with drinking. And I began to look forward to going home to 'make-love' to my bottle. I was beginning to think and act a bit less than normal.

"Since the kids were becoming independent, my husband focused more on me and my drinking — and, he complained. I became irritated, and actually justified my drinking as a necessary and deserving way of coping with his incessant criticism. Although I began to question my drinking, everybody still thought I was not an alcoholic. In fact, I guess my husband got burned out from complaining without support because he soon joined me in drinking. For several years we would both get buzzed together. So my husband also had a drinking problem.

"During this heavier drinking period, I still continued to function relatively well. I never missed a day of work, never got caught breaking the law, continued to progress in my profession, and became an administrator in my forties.

"My oldest son, Paul, had an alcoholic problem himself in his sophomore year. After his life began to fall apart, like falling grades, being busted for drunken driving, and overall oppositional behavior, we pressured him to enter a rehab program. Fortunately, my son was one of the success stories. He worked and is working a twelve step program and has grown in sobriety. I'm proud of him.

"My other two kids grew up without obvious scars, and all three went to college, graduated with high grades, and got good jobs. However, two of them have had marital problems, which they seem to be working on. In fact, one of them is working an ACOA (Adult Children of Alcoholics) program. You see that although alcoholism did not seem to impede my public and work life, there were consequences in my personal life.

"I had many enablers, and the chief ones were my husband and parents. For instance, my husband would buy me alcohol, join me in drinking, and for a long time gave the impression that my drinking was okay. I can understand why he would enable, for he is an adult child of an alcoholic mother, and besides we had great times when we were high.

"Loved ones simply enabled me by denying my alcoholism. And I could always count on them for several half gallons of fine whiskey at Christmas and my birthday. In any case, I was the proverbial elephant in the living room whom everyone walked around while pretending that it did not exist. Most of all, they loved and tried to care for me.

"To this very day, none of my relatives and friends would say that I am an alcoholic. In fact, I was an average drinker compared to many of them. In our collusive self-deception, we fooled one another. Still, we had good times. Now that I have become sober for seven years, many of my friends who still drink have become somewhat distant with me. It can be difficult to be together when one is drinking and the other is not. Although we are still friends, we are different friends. I could go on and on, but more importantly, how did I come to recovery?

"What happened was that my chief enabler, John, my husband, became my chief non-enabler and therapeutic agent. John told me that when he was drinking heavily with me, he hit his bottom, which scared him so much that he sought help. Besides getting dry, he, on the advice of a friend, began to go to Al-Anon meetings. With the help of the Al-Anon fellowship and its 12-step program, John began to deal with his own problems — not so much alcoholism but co-alcoholism and ACOA issues. He learned to take care of himself and to detach from alcoholism. My husband's renewed life made a tremendous impact on me.

"Our marital relationship changed radically. No longer did John enable me, but rather he let me be responsible for the consequences of my drinking. At first, I was glad that John backed off, but eventually I began to feel anxious, then guilty, and ultimately ashamed. For some reason, being left on my own with my drinking was more difficult. John was moving forward, with or without me, and his happiness and freedom confused and scared me. So, I would show him and the world; I would cut down on my drinking. And I did.

"I quit drinking for a four month period, but resumed drinking again. In fact, for three years I was a periodic drinker. I would stop for three or four months and start to drink secretly on weekends. Although I decreased the amount of drinking and changed my drinking patterns, I still looked forward to my weekend rendezvous. Instead of seeing my lover (alcohol) everyday, I saw him on weekends.

"My white knuckle approach was difficult, but the difficulty sent me a message, namely: that I was not as free or in control of my drinking as I once thought. For example, it was difficult for me not to drink on weekends. And although I would quit drinking for several months, I always seemed to return. Looking back, I realize that knowing the future — that I could always drink — enabled me to abstain for awhile.

"By this time, I knew that I had a drinking problem, but neither I nor most people would call myself an alcoholic. Still in time I found myself reading about alcoholism and entertaining the possibility that I might be an alcoholic. I had to admit that I was sneaking drinks, that I was hiding the bottle, that I thought too much about drinking, that I had hangovers, that I was using mouthwash, that I put up a sober front, etc. But I rationalized that since I did not drink during the week, could abstain for months, and managed well, I was not alcoholic.

"I reasoned that I never drank in the morning, never went to bars, never missed work, never got in trouble with the law, never got really drunk, never became dysfunctional, never got sick, never got violent, that my friends were heavier drinkers, that I was usually the designated driver, that I was responsible, that I managed, that I was a nice woman, etc., etc., etc. — all true, but not the whole truth. I later learned that being adamant about control is an indicator of alcoholism.

"Still, I came to admit, albeit from the neck up, that I looked forward to being pleasantly high and that drinking played too much a part of my life. So, just to be honest or to prove to myself that I was not an alcoholic, I went to an A.A. meeting. That night I heard a lead story that was far removed from my own story. This person got a divorce, lost his kids, got violent, lost his job, was jailed, and had hit a very low bottom. When he said that his worst day sober was better than his best day drinking, it just didn't ring true to me. I was different! Surely, I was not one of them. I just didn't feel at home at this A.A. meeting. Thus, when I returned home, I had more evidence that I was not a true alcoholic.

"One night — a night I'll never forget — my husband took me to a fine restaurant as part of my birthday present. Before we left, I had one stiff Manhattan — my last drink. (I can still taste it.) When we were about to enter the restaurant, he stopped and asked: 'Mary, have you been drinking?' I responded, 'Not at all, why do you ask? I haven't had a drink. Do you want to smell my breath?' John simply responded, 'No, I just thought I smelled alcohol on your breath and wanted to point that out.' I think the fact that John just accepted me had a more devastating effect on me than if he would have become critical or argumentative.

"At that moment I felt a shame that I had never felt before

in my life. I felt that I had lied and covered up, was betraying my husband, and moreso myself. The truth of my alcoholic drinking engulfed me. During dinner, I had trouble concentrating and enjoying my meal as well as looking at my husband and with him looking at me. I felt overwhelming shame. I felt painfully diminished; I felt like disappearing for life. For whatever reason, I drank no more.

"For the next two-and-a-half-months I remained dry and became a bit sober. And there were no perceivable or felt physical consequences from not drinking. Although I did this many times before, this time I abstained mainly out of fear and shame, not pride and arrogance. Seldom was drinking much of a temptation then or since then, for I knew that I was better off not drinking. Anyhow, I did not drink, but my abstinence was initially a solo flight, that is: without others and God.

"Finally, I mustered the courage to go back to an A.A. meeting. I'm sure I got the courage because of my husband's as well as God's gentle but persistent nudging. Like the first meeting two years earlier, I did not feel at home. I heard another lead story that was far different than my own story, and unfortunately no one really welcomed me at the meeting. I went to another meeting, and again the lead was not that pertinent to me, although a few points resonated within me. I think the speaker evoked my shame. And again only one person welcomed me. I felt out of place. Because of these experiences, I now welcome and take special interest in new members.

"Today I feel more in place and I know that I belong in A.A. because the program is not only a good program for me, an alcoholic, but also is a good program for living. I have made great friends, gotten a sponsor, and feel more at home, but never quite like many seem to feel — totally comfortable. Maybe it's because as a child, I felt wanted and secure at home, but nowhere else. Or maybe alcoholics like myself don't fit A.A. quite as well as other alcoholics. Or maybe I'm fooling myself. Whatever the case, I continue to be grateful to A.A.

"I continued to go to three meetings a week, and after about nine months, I heard a lead from a woman who was a closet, homemaker alcoholic. She would only drink between 4:00 and 6:00 p.m. and when she socialized. Finally, I heard a story that was mine. In fact, it seemed like she drank less than I, but nevertheless identified herself as an alcoholic and was active in the program for ten years. She touched me.

"As time went on, I began to share more, albeit cautiously, with my husband, and our marriage became healthier and more intimate. I experienced the difference between living sober and living with alcohol. Slowly but surely, I admitted, accepted, and surrendered to the fact that I was and am an alcoholic, albeit functional, controlled, or whatever name you want to call it. In fact, I developed a simple definition of alcoholism that seems to fit me. I saw and see alcoholism as a process of drinking that harms your life more than it helps. And I finally admit that drinking harmed me more than it helped me.

"When I truly did admit that I was an alcoholic, I experienced tremendous relief. Nevertheless, for a couple of years the demons of doubt would still question me. And my drinking friends and family members also doubt or simply do not accept that I am an alcoholic. I understand their reluctance, for I was at least as normal as anyone else and often better off. In fact, most people thought that my husband was an alcoholic because he was a public and boisterous drinker whereas I was a secret mellow drinker. Now, however, I can accept that I am an alcoholic and live with that fact.

"I have learned to value my pain as an important source of truth that enables me to be aware, to cope, and to grow. Actually, my pain is often a saving grace. For instance, when I used to feel afraid, frustrated, or angry, I would alcoholize my feelings. Now I listen to and learn from them. To be sure, I don't like pain, but paradoxically I am grateful for my pain.

"Overall, I am more fully alive and more wholly a human being. I am simply running a better race. Although I'd like to live a long and sober life, I am no longer ashamed to die, for I know now that I can die with integrity and dignity"

Mary's story and others like it can serve as a basis and springboard for our discussion and analysis of normal alcoholism. Most types of alcoholism are cunning, baffling, and powerful. Some alcoholisms may be even more insidious and difficult to detect and accept. As Mary's story demonstrates, her alcoholism, like most forms, was very easy to rationalize, deny, and enable. And although such alcoholism disrupts and hurts people's lives, it is not usually blatantly dysfunctional or unmanageable, and consequently more normal than abnormal. Indeed, to most people Mary was a model mother, successful worker, and a concerned and responsible individual. Few would say that she was (is) an alcoholic. Although common, alcoholisms like Mary's can easily go unaddressed and untreated.

Like Mary, most alcoholics seldom enter treatment and/or A.A. programs. Instead, they are more likely to drink their entire lives, or for various reasons eventually curtail or quit drinking, but not really become sober. They remain "dry alcoholics." Furthermore, many alcoholics live useful and good lives, but probably not as useful and as good as they could with sobriety. Indeed, many publicly influential people, like politicians, writers, artists, lawyers, doctors, and ministers, have been alcoholic. And many ordinary people have also lived significant but alcoholic lives. If you doubt this statement, keep reading and thinking.

His Story

"I took my last drink seven years ago on my fifty-fifth birthday, and with the exception of periodic abstinence, I drank alcoholically for thirty-six years. Yet, few people accept that I am an alcoholic, for, you see, I was a very successful and public person.

"Realize that drinking and over-drinking was the norm in

my family. My family would ask a nondrinker what's wrong rather than what's right. Thus, I grew up with heavy drinking, particularly at times of celebration like weddings, funerals, holidays, birthdays, or whatever special occasion. My expectations to be an adult as well as how to celebrate included abnormal drinking, which we felt was normal. The abnormal was the norm.

"Since I was a bright kid and leader, I did well in and out of school. Life — school, work, play, friends, parents — came easy. In fact, I look back on my childhood with fond memories. I played a lot and had fun, and home was always a safe and good place to be. And I worked hard, starting at seven with a paper route followed by setting up pins, caddying, and being a stock boy, and at sixteen I worked during the summer 40 hours a week in a steel mill. I was already a workaholic like my lovable workaholic father. Still, to my credit, I worked hard, saved money, and to that extent was disciplined and dedicated.

"Even though I seldom drank in high school, my drinking seemed different than most of my peers. I can recall one New Year's Eve when my parents went to a party, three friends and I had our own party. We drank beer, whiskey, and wine. Unexpectedly, my parents and their friends returned home around 12:20 and caught us flying high. Interestingly, two of my friends went staggering home immediately, and my other friend was very sick. However, I became relatively sober, made up excuses for me and my friends, and gained control and took charge of our drunken situation. What I also remember of those two or three adolescent drinking bouts is that it felt natural.

"Although in high school I was a B student with little studying, in college I became somewhat compulsive about academic achievement and graduated fourth in my class. In college my drinking was scheduled so that it didn't interfere with my studies. Typically, on Friday and some Saturday evenings, I would drink to the extent of getting a buzz, but I never drank during the week. The important thing was that I liked and looked forward to getting buzzed; it felt right.

"To be analytic, I'm sure that alcohol loosened up my compulsive tendencies and enabled me to relax and feel mellow. I felt relaxed and free when I drank. Still, my drinking was limited to Friday and Saturday evenings; on Sunday I started studying again. And, being a good worker and succeeding so well academically enabled me to deny the subtle insanity of my emerging alcoholism.

"My dad and I had a lot of enjoyable times drinking together. We would often work on projects together, and after work, we would drink, talk, and have good warm times. And my mother would never say her husband and son were alcoholics. To her, an alcoholic was someone who lost control and was an embarrassment. Her men worked hard, and were good men. She was proud of us.

"For whatever reasons, since my junior year in high school, I had this crazy notion that maybe priesthood was something I should look into. Maybe it was my parents' Irish influence, or the good nuns and brothers, or perhaps it appealed to my perfectionist and co-dependent personality, maybe it was an avoidance of intimacy, or maybe God was calling me. So, in my senior year I decided to give it a shot — to get it deeper in or out of my system.

"I'll skip my seminary days. Suffice it to say, my drinking was on the shelf except during the holidays and home visits when I got an opportunity to drink. But no one ever questioned me about drinking, let alone alcoholism. Understandably so, practically everyone drank, and besides, such a 'good seminarian' who drank less than many could never be an alcoholic. Anyhow, I continued to excel academically, earned a Master's in theology, was ordained, got high after my ordination party, went on a drinking vacation, and was assigned to a parish with an alcoholic pastor. Smooth as silk.

"Although people suspected that my pastor was an alcoholic, they covered up for him because he was a good man who didn't cause any trouble, and besides, the parish was in solid financial condition. At this assignment, I became a moderate drinker, fully living, dynamic, effective, and compassionate priest. In many ways, I was on top of the world. Some parishioners not only called me Father Peter, but covertly, St. Peter. But like St. Peter, my self-will was running rampant and I was increasingly less dependent on God. Of course, I administered the sacraments and celebrated daily Mass, but my spiritual life was dissipating.

"My next two assignments were with troubled priests. I became known as one of the diocesan trouble shooters — those priests who put a parish in order without officially being the pastor. God gave me a number of gifts, and one of them was being a successful administrator as well as an effective minister and homilist. Little did people know that an alcoholic was taking care of others. I functioned very well.

"Although I managed my duties efficiently, related well with people, and had friends, my life of intimacy was lacking. I was an expert at listening to and helping others, but rarely if ever did I share myself on a personal level. I was a good helper, but I would never let myself be helped. Although I never got sexually involved with a woman — thank God — I came close on several occasions, and understandably so. I would cope with my desire for intimacy and my loneliness by nurturing and numbing myself with alcohol. Rather than helping me cope with and grow from these issues, my drinking only exacerbated them. The more I drank, the lonelier I got. Alcoholism simply is not an adequate substitute for people and God.

"Although few if any people knew that I was alcoholic, they knew I liked to drink, for every Christmas I was given many bottles of booze. One Christmas I received 47 bottles of the finest spirits. Although the etymology of alcohol means spirit, I don't think the bottles, even the Chivas Regal, contained the Holy Spirit. If they had, I would have been well on my way to sainthood.

"Anyhow, I finally became a pastor of my own parish. And true to my script, I moved quickly, established important contacts, and began to make significant changes. In two and a half years, the parish grew from a relatively dead community to one that was spirited and financially sound. During this time, I maintained my drinking, namely two to three drinks at cocktail hour and two or more at night. At forty-four I had achieved what I wanted — to be recognized as a successful and good pastor. Yet I felt like there was nothing more to motivate me.

"I continued to do a fine job. I was still mentally quick with my responses, as dynamic in my homilies, and almost as compassionate as I had been. Although I was drinking too much, I still managed to manage. At a distance (where I kept almost everyone), I looked competent and compassionate, so at least: normal. But my spiritual life was at a low point. Rarely did I pray, say the office, or even do spiritual reading. I did read, but only to keep informed of the latest theories and current events that would help me be a good homilist and minister. Seldom did I read for spiritual formation, but primarily for information. I progressively got out of touch with myself and to some extent became a caricature of myself.

"Then when I was fifty-five years old, my day of infamy came. I finally broke down, which enabled me to break through. As always, I quit drinking during Lent, but this time I started to drink heavily Easter Saturday afternoon and by late evening crossed the line. I was the main celebrant for Easter Vigil service. I still shudder with a smile and get embarrassed when I think of it. O *felix culpa!*

"I can recall standing outside our Church lighting the Easter Vigil fire to symbolize the Light of Christ shining through the darkness. Well, I used far too much lighter fluid and started a fire that almost got out of control. Not that this was so bad, but I began to giggle and mumble: '*Resurrexit, sicut dixit. Alleluia!*' My associates looked at me with anxious concern, and managed to get a fire extinguisher.

"Walking into the church, singing the *Lumen Christi*, I began to stagger. Hopefully not too many recognized my less than smooth gait, but the people in procession with me did. For the first time, I was getting out of control in public. I began to get scared and tried to sober up, but I couldn't. Yuck! What a feeling! What grace! Upon reaching the altar and under the influences of alcohol, incense, and a packed, stuffy church, I got physically sick and nauseous. I felt a strong urge to throw up, and I did. Fortunately, I turned around and missed the altar. My fellow priests ushered me out and made an announcement that I had become ill. Most people accepted this excuse, but the fact was that I was drunk, soused, caput!

"The next morning I apologized to my confreres and said that I must have eaten some tainted food. One of my associates said that I may have had too much to drink, but I denied it. Anyhow, although I did have a hangover, I managed to function at the two other Masses. Later in the day, I went to dinner at my brother's house where I had several drinks to ease my frayed nerves. My brother said that he heard I was sick at midnight Mass, and I assured him that I must have had a touch of the flu. Again, none of the family members confronted me about my drinking.

"However, the following week I had my time of resurrection. On the Thursday after Easter, a friend invited me for lunch, and when I entered his rectory, there were three other friends as well as a person whom I respected — namely my first pastor who was now in his late seventies. In short, they along with a drug counselor conducted an intervention. Each one of them with compassion and without resentment pointed out to me how my drinking behavior was causing disruption and harm to myself and others. At first, I vehemently disagreed with them and countered with my achievements. Rather than arguing with me, they simply pointed out concrete instances of my alcoholic behavior.

"Then I became angry at them for not agreeing with me. Again, instead of arguing or reacting, they were compassionate. I started to get scared. I admitted to having a bit too much alcohol on occasion, but was quick to point out that many people do this and I have always done well. Trying to show good will, I bargained with them promising that I would get help from a counselor or even go to A.A. if I continued such a drinking pattern. Instead of bargaining with me, they encouraged me to admit that I had a serious drinking problem and should enter a treatment center for alcoholic priests.

"For some reason or another, I began to break down and sob. Gathering around and comforting me, they promised to help and stand by me. I felt deeply humiliated and humbled. I also felt accepted and loved. For the first time in my life, I came clean. At this time I didn't know if I was alcoholic or not, but I did know that my drinking was not healthy.

"Anyhow, that evening I was on a plane to enter a treatment program for alcoholic priests. I stayed for five months. I am lucky, for most inpatient rehabs only last a month, and I needed more time. When I returned from the rehab, I was on the road to sobriety.

"My parishioners assumed that I was away for studies and medical rejuvenation, and I told them I was away to recuperate from being ill. I let the story be general and for the most part people accepted it. Although I would not lie about my alcoholism, I would tell people what I thought was best for them and myself, and if saying I am an alcoholic was best, that's what I'd say. Really, people were not so much interested in what was wrong with me, but how I acted now.

"After rehab, I worked my 90-90 program — 90 meetings in 90 days. I still go to several meetings a week. As I initially worked my twelve step program, it was important to admit being alcoholic, but even more importantly, I realized that I could live a better life without drinking. In fact only after a year of being dry and sober, I could see big differences between my drinking and non-drinking lives, such as having more energy, functioning better and more consistently, and enjoying life much more. No longer did I fall asleep at 10:00 and wake up at 12:00. Now I stay alert as well as sleep better. And although I was always a good worker, I became a better worker, a better priest, a better person.

"My spiritual life with God and friends has also improved. Now, my vows and loneliness motivate me to live a virtuous life. I am learning, one day at a time, to be a chaste and compassionate man who can give and receive in ways that truly foster priesthood. I pray daily for the grace to accept and the courage to follow God's way. Paradoxically, I function more efficiently, enjoy life more, and am freer since I am more dependent on God.

"I became a sober pastor rather than an alcoholic pastor. No longer do I feel that I am a caricature of myself or simply a functional priest; now my heart is in it. I'm learning to live what I used to preach; I really experience God in myself and others. What a difference that makes. What a revelation, what a liberation, what a reconciliation!

"In looking back, I can see that my alcoholism began subtly in childhood, with some symptoms in high school, and a bit more in college. In the seminary, my alcoholism escalated not in actual drinking, but in my attitude of looking forward to drinking. After ordination, I graduated to vodka martinis — less obvious to the olfactory nerves. My drinking progressed to the two drink cocktail hour and more in the evening when my work day was over. Along with Lenten abstinence and vacation binges, I consistently maintained this schedule for more than three decades.

"I am now working with our diocese to formulate a program that includes ways to intervene and help troubled priests. In fact, I think this program should begin in the seminaries — to teach future priests to diagnose, cope with, intervene, and help alcoholic priests. And such education would also enable us to help the laity. There are many good people — priests and laity — who are holy and alcoholic. Instead of denying or enabling their disorder, our ministry calls us to help them become holy and sober."

Father Peter, like many alcoholics, managed and succeeded as well as and often better than others. He was responsible and accountable, and he never got into any civil or canonical trouble. His pastoral and liturgical ministry, homilies, administrative skills, and overall demeanor were admired. And besides, people trusted and liked him. Nevertheless, the most important dimension of both his personal and professional life — his spiritual life, was neglected. Rather than facing and nourishing himself in healthy ways, he took care of his starving spirit with alcohol. In a sense, this priest tried to displace God (the Holy Spirit) with alcohol (spirits). Consequently, the hole in his soul expanded, and he became less than his true self. Still, he was a good and holy man. Now, he is a better, healthier, and holier man.

For most of their adult lives, Mary and Peter were normal alcoholics. Despite being alcoholic, they maintained reasonable control of themselves, got along with and helped others, were effective workers, met their responsibilities, managed the consequences of drinking, and were good persons. Their drinking rarely got out of control, nor was it socially or legally disruptive. They were not as powerless over alcohol as some alcoholics. But only after decades of alcoholic drinking did a few people recognize their alcoholism. Only after they, particularly Peter, lost blatant control, was therapeutic action taken. "Why" and "how" Mary and Peter were and are alcoholics, along with millions of people like them, is the topic of this book.

2 Perspectives on Alcoholism

Listen to this embellished anecdote. While studying Freudian psychology in graduate school, I worked in a psychiatric hospital. I was amazed at how so many patients were orally dependent, anally obsessive, had dire interpersonal problems that reflected Oedipal enmeshments, or had weak egos as a result of instinctual flooding and regression. I clearly saw that therapeutic goals included working through these fixations and repressions while increasing ego strength. Psychology, I smugly thought, really seemed to make sense.

The following year I studied the works of Alfred Adler. For some strange reason, my patients seemed to change. It seemed now that patients were guilty of erring with a lifestyle of self-centeredness and willpower rather than fostering social concern. It was evident, at least to me, that they had been so pampered or were so insecure in childhood that they had to overcompensate and control others to deal with their inadequacy. A therapeutic goal was to help them actualize their healthy "creative self" by learning genuine concern for others.

My "Adlerian patients," however, seemed to change again when I studied the writings of Carl Jung. Now my patients were clearly manifesting the dark side of their personality — the primitive and passionate energy that we inherit not only from our individual history but from humankind. My challenge was to help them face their shadow as well as other latent archetypes, use this energy for constructive behavior, and foster their individualization to become balanced, self-actualizing, whole persons. Amen!

However, the following year it seemed I no longer saw Freudian, Adlerian, and Jungian patients, for I began to see people that were in a state of incongruence between their experience and their self-concept, and what they needed was to express and process their feelings. Following the model of Carl Rogers, I assumed that my clients were basically good so that I only needed to accept and understand them, and with unconditional positive regard reflect their feelings. Furthermore, since my clients knew what was best for them, I could trust them to act appropriately. Ah, becoming healthy seemed so simple.

After Rogers, I began to study the theories of Karen Horney, and of course, my patients changed again. I could see that reflecting feelings was not enough. We had to work through their basic anxiety, helplessness, and hostility that were usually rooted in the basic evil of neurotic child rearing. Instead of fixating in defensive styles of only moving toward, away or against others, my goal included helping them develop an open and flexible style that would engender security and freedom, defuse anger, and increase self-worth. Rather than futilely try to be an ideal, perfect self, their challenge was to accept and become their real, limited self. Life was more complex than Rogerian theorists would contend, but nevertheless understandable.

Then I was transferred to a unit where the resident doctor operated a token economy program. I learned that it was not necessary to work through the past, deal with intrapsychic and interpersonal dynamics, or even process feelings, but rather it was more important to deal with what you can observe and measure — behavior. My primary goal was to reinforce behavior by giving tokens which were needed to gain privileges. This action-oriented and scientific approach also made sense.

Along with this behavioral approach, I learned how important it was to help patients be aware of and improve their cognitive processes. I appreciated how patients' attitudes and beliefs highly influence how they act; consequently, changing their attitudes and beliefs could change their behavior. If you follow realistic thinking, you behave appropriately. Once again, I felt I had a good grasp of how to help people.

After graduating, I was seeing a patient who seemed very angry. I asked her what she was angry about, and she responded: "You!" She stated that she had been trying to share an important experience of intimacy, and I seemed insistent on focusing on loneliness and encouraging her to cry. I suddenly realized that I was imposing my own particular theory on her, for at that time I was writing a book about how loneliness can lead to growth. I apologized and quickly bracketed my theories so I could listen to and understand what *she* was experiencing, not I.

The purpose of this facetious story is to emphasize how easy it is to operate as if people are in service of theories instead of using theories in service of people. Actually, my clinical and academic supervisors curbed my well-intentioned therapeutic manipulation and helped me to learn from such experiences. Indeed, I am still careful of trying to control and change people according to my particular gospels.

Nevertheless, all approaches shed some light on people, and particular theories lend themselves more to some people than to others. A psychodynamic approach of Freud, Adler, Horney, or Jung might be more helpful to some patients than other approaches. Still other patients may benefit more from an affective approach like Gestalt or client-centered counseling; whereas others may find a cognitive/behavioral or reality therapy more beneficial. And often a patient benefits from more than one approach. Rather than manipulating people to fit a theory, my approach is to let them call forth the theories that help them improve their lives.

Similar to the field of personality theory, there are many theories of alcoholism, and some approaches explain and treat certain alcoholics better than others. For instance a medical/disease model of alcoholism may be more useful to some alcoholics than to others. The point is that instead of rigidly applying one model, our goal is to use the models that are most effective to the particular alcoholic in question.

A primary thesis is that the way we construe alcoholism highly determines the way we diagnose, treat, and feel about alcoholism. Therefore, it is important for us to know consciously and clearly our personal views (theories, beliefs, assumptions, expectations) toward drinking. Keep in mind, all of us hold theories about alcoholism which may be more or less helpful and/or harmful.

For instance, if we view an alcoholic only as one who is on skid row, frequently drunk, out of control, and blatantly disruptive and embarrassing, then our theory of alcoholism needs to be modified. Although such a view includes some alcoholics, it excludes most of them and therefore precludes helping them. Instead of one "alcoholism," there are many "alcoholisms." And instead of one theory, there are many theories and treatments.

Unfortunately, we tend to take our personal and professional theories for granted and seldom put them to the test of honest reflection, empirical data, or dialogue. For example, if you believe that love, honesty, and open communication will change an alcoholic, you are sooner or later going to experience frustration, exhaustion, anger, and possible depression because such a belief/model is not entirely accurate. Although genuine care and acceptance are recommended, probably necessary, and usually increase the likelihood of recovery, they cannot change others. In fact, such co-dependent motivation and behavior can enable alcoholic behavior.

In short, the way we view alcoholism co-constitutes the meaning that alcoholism has for us, and therefore highly influences how we experience, judge, treat, cope with, feel about, and live with alcoholics. The purpose of this chapter is to present some relatively well-known and used approaches toward alcoholism to help us reflect on the way we view and treat alcoholics.

A.A. Model

Most drug counselors as well as recovering addicts would agree that the most accepted and effective ongoing treatment of addiction is the twelve step program of Alcoholics Anonymous. In fact, treatment facilities for addictive (and co-addictive) disorders invariably incorporate the A.A. approach in their residential, after care, and outpatient programs. And most people have heard about Alcoholics Anonymous, for it has burgeoned in scholarly and popular literature, mass media, and self-help groups. But what makes A.A. so appealing?

A.A. is unique in that it offers a structured, wholistic, and communal approach toward recovery that promises alcoholics, with few exceptions, a sober and better life. Its structure centers on twelve steps, traditions, and concepts. First of all, the steps — the way to recovery — emphasize acceptance of one's powerlessness over alcohol, dependency on a Higher Power, a personal inventory and reconciliation, spiritual exercises, and the promise to practice the steps throughout life. Whereas the steps focus on recovery, the traditions guide and safeguard A.A.'s harmony and unity. With recovery and unity, the mission of service, which is proclaimed in the concepts, completes the triangular framework of A.A. — recovery, unity, and service.

Secondly, the A.A. approach is also wholistic in that it integrates biomedical, psychosocial, and spiritual principles of recovery. Unlike other treatment approaches, A.A. synthesizes biomedical/physical perspectives toward alcoholism, psychosocial principles of communication and coping, and spiritual practices of transcendence, virtue, and healing.

And thirdly, this structured and wholistic approach is implemented and lived in the context of community. With the acceptance, understanding, and guidance of A.A. fellowship, meetings, and personal sponsorship, alcoholics are continually invited out of their isolation and in to being with and for others — a key dynamic of recovery.

Although A.A. is primarily a spiritual program that fosters surrendering to a Power greater than one's individual self, A.A. emphasizes that it is not a religion. Rather, A.A. is a spiritual approach that encourages turning one's will and life over to the care of God as one understands God. Although this spiritual reality is usually called God, it can be any useful and greater Power and/or care such as the A.A. fellowship, nature, love, or any reality that goes beyond and includes one's individuality. In the context of this personal and communal spiritual reality, A.A. members share their transgressions, make amends for them, and help themselves and one another to nurture and realize their positive potentials. So, how does A.A. view alcoholism?

Although there may be as many conceptions of alcoholism in A.A. as there are alcoholics, our concern is the model of alcoholism as found in the A.A. literature and tradition as well as in most twelve step programs like Al-Anon, Families Anonymous, Adult Children of Alcoholics, Co-dependents Anonymous, and POTADA (Parents of Teenage Alcohol and Drug Abusers). Such fellowships usually view alcoholism as a disease that is comparable to other diseases like diabetes or as similar to an allergy. To this extent A.A. primarily adopts a medical model.

A.A. considers alcoholism to be a *primary* disease in that it is not symptomatic of another more basic disease, *chronic* in that it will never disappear, *progressive* in that it will worsen with continued drinking, and *fatal* in that it eventually leads to dysfunctional and/or institutionalized living or premature death. Since A.A. takes the position that alcoholism cannot be cured, an alcoholic can never drink successfully. But paradoxically, although A.A.'s diagnosis is medical, its treatment is primarily spiritual, secondarily psychosocial, and seldom (after detoxification) medical.

Bill Wilson, a co-founder of A.A. and the chief author of *Alcoholics Anonymous*, points out that an essential dynamic of alcoholics in contrast to so-called moderate hard drinkers is that alcoholics lose control of alcohol once they start to drink (*Alco-*

holics Anonymous, pp. 18-24). As A.A. members say: "One drink is too many and a thousand is not enough." Instead of controlling the alcohol, the alcohol controls them. To complicate matters, alcoholics are experts at denial and are apt to delude themselves into thinking that they can control their drinking; in fact, they are out of control.

Faithful to his principles and personality, Wilson remains open to other ways of thinking or at least exceptions when he reaffirms the basic A.A. approach as follows: "We alcoholics are men and women who have lost the ability to control our drinking. We know that no real alcoholic ever reaches control. All of us felt at times we were regaining control, but such intervals — usually brief — were inevitably followed by less control, which led in time to pitiful and incomprehensible demoralization. We are convinced that alcoholics of our type are in the grip of a progressive illness. Over any considerable period we get worse, never better" (*Alcoholics Anonymous*, p. 30).

When Wilson states that "alcoholics of our type" lose control, he allows for the possibility of alcoholics who may not lose control or progress while drinking. As we will see, our model of normal alcoholism might have been accepted by Bill Wilson, Bob Smith, and other founders of A.A., and certainly can be incorporated into the A.A. philosophy. Nevertheless, the official stance and usual practice of A.A. include admitting powerlessness over alcohol, unmanageableness, progression, chronicity and therefore complete abstinence. Our project is to respond to Wilson's invitation by not refuting A.A.'s concept of alcoholism but by building on it.

Jellinek's Model

A seminal and significant study is E.N. Jellinek's *The Disease Concept of Alcoholism* (1960). In his ground-breaking work, Jellinek differentiates five basic kinds of alcoholism: Alpha, Beta,

Gamma, Delta, and Epsilon (pp. 35-41). To increase our understanding of alcoholism, let us reflect on the following summary of these alcoholisms.

The first type of alcoholism, *alpha alcoholism*, Jellinek describes as a purely psychological and continual reliance upon the effect of alcohol to relieve bodily or emotional pain. Although alpha drinkers are "undisciplined," they seldom "lose control," and they maintain an "ability to abstain." Furthermore, the consequences of alpha alcoholism are unlikely to include seriously disruptive loss, but are likely to center on interpersonal relationships, monetary problems, occasional absenteeism from work, decreased productivity, and some nutritional deficiencies. A key factor is that alpha alcoholics are not physically dependent on alcohol so that there are no disturbances due to alcohol withdrawal nor are these signs of a progressive process.

Since alpha alcoholics use alcohol to relieve physical and emotional discomfort, their alcohol abuse is indicative of an underlying condition which alcohol hides and anesthetizes. Alpha alcoholics use alcohol primarily to cope with and relieve the discomfort of problems, while managing their lives relatively well. Jellinek states that although alpha alcoholism cannot be regarded as a disease per se, it can lead to the disease of gamma alcoholism. Particularly interesting to our thesis is Jellinek's observation that alpha alcoholism may be seen in a drinking career of twenty or forty years without signs of progression. Alpha alcoholism would support our model of normal alcoholism.

Beta alcoholism involves medical complications such as gastritis, hepatitis, pancreatitis, and cirrhosis of the liver and yet does not include physical or psychological dependence upon alcohol. In a sense, beta alcoholics have an allergy to alcohol and/or cannot tolerate alcohol. For instance, certain oriental people, although not obsessed with and compelled to drink, become drastically sick when they drink alcohol. Beta alcoholism may also develop into gamma alcoholism, but not as likely as alpha alcoholism.

Gamma alcoholism is the classic chronic alcoholism found most frequently in A.A. and in adult treatment programs. According to Jellinek (1960, pp. 37-38), gamma alcoholism is a disease because it incorporates an acquired increase of tissue tolerance to alcohol (takes more to produce the same effect), adaptive cell metabolism, withdrawal symptoms, craving (physical dependence), and loss of control that significantly impairs interpersonal relations, economic, social and recreational activities, work, intimacy, spirituality — life. Gamma alcoholism would often be more abnormal than normal.

Delta alcoholism is a class of alcoholism that is peculiar to some cultures. For instance, delta alcoholics can be found in wine growing countries like France, where they drink wine daily and with control. Although delta alcoholics have "an inability to abstain," they maintain control and function "normally" while drinking daily. Although they lack the control to quit drinking, they manage to cope well. For them, to be normal is to drink.

In contrast, *epsilon alcoholism* primarily involves "periodic alcoholism." Actually, such alcoholism is constantly latent and periodically activated. For instance, epsilon alcoholics typically resist drinking for weeks, months, or even years, and then relapse often until they collapse, and eventually and remorsefully return to abstinence. This cycle between normal and abnormal behavior is recurrent.

Jellinek (pg. 39) briefly describes other types of alcoholism, such as "explosive drinking," "excessive weekend drinking," and "fiesta drinking." He also warns us that other forms of alcoholism cannot and should not be overlooked. Jellinek (pp. 39-40) concludes that alpha and epsilon alcoholisms can be ruled out as diseases in that they are symptomatic of an underlying disturbance as well as beta alcoholism which is not a disease per se. Only gamma and delta alcoholisms can be considered diseases.

Important to our study is that alpha alcoholics manage relatively well. Also in contrast to gamma alcoholics, delta alcoholics lack the typical urge to abstain or control, and their ability to control the amount on any given occasion remains intact. For our purpose, these alpha and delta alcoholics can be considered normal alcoholics.

Although published in 1960, Jellinek's analyses of different as well as cross-cultural kinds of alcoholism are provocative and informative. One of his contentions was that although alcoholism is usually considered to be an addiction of the type that is prevalent in A.A., there are many kinds of alcoholics who never become addicted in the classical sense. To affirm the various forms of alcoholism, Jellinek gives the following definition while admitting that it is operationally vague: Alcoholism is "any use of alcoholic beverages that causes any damage to the individual or both" (pg. 35). Although not the same, this definition is congruent with our model of alcoholism.

DSM-IV Model

A third model of alcoholism is taken from the American Psychiatric Association's *Diagnostic and Statistic Manual of Mental Disorders*, fourth edition. The psychiatric nosologies, syndromes, and analyses presented in this book are usually used in the U.S.A. for diagnostic and/or insurance purposes. Although various treatment approaches may be used, the DSM-IV criteria are used to justify third party payment for in- and outpatient treatment.

Alcoholism is one of the substance-related disorders, of which there are two basic categories: substance use disorder and substance-induced disorders. And substance use disorders consist of two types: substance (alcohol) dependence and substance (alcohol) abuse. To quote DSM-IV, substance (alcohol) dependence is essentially characterized by "a cluster of cognitive, behavioral, and physiological symptoms indicating that the individual continues use of the substance despite substance-related problems. There is a pattern of repeated self-administration that usually results in tolerance, withdrawal, and compulsive drug taking behavior (DSM-IV, p. 176).

Alcohol dependence is diagnosed when three or more of the following signs or symptoms occur at any time in the same twelve month period. Tolerance, a common symptom, refers to either a need for significantly increased amounts of alcohol to achieve the desired effect or a markedly diminished effect with continued alcohol use. For example, dependent alcoholics need to drink more to attain the effects that they once achieved with less alcohol. Another key diagnostic factor is withdrawal which is described as a maladaptive behavioral change, with physiological and cognitive concomitants, that occurs when blood or tissue concentrations of alcohol decline in a person who has maintained heavy use. When dependent alcoholics undergo withdrawal symptoms, they are likely to drink to relieve or avoid the unpleasant symptoms. "To take a hair of the dog that bit them" is a sign of withdrawal. Although physiological dependence on alcohol is indicated by evidence of tolerance or withdrawal, it is possible to be dependent on alcohol without physiological dependence (DSM-IV, pp. 176-177).

A third indicator of alcohol dependence is taking larger amounts of alcohol over a longer period of time than one intended. For example, a person intends to drink no more than two two-ounce drinks per day but fails to keep his promise by frequently drinking more. Fourthly, a person experiences persistent desires and/or successful efforts to decrease or control alcohol use. Despite the best of intentions and rigorous efforts to decrease his consumption, the alcoholic dependent at best maintains and usually increases his alcohol intake. Or fifth, a person continues drinking despite an awareness of persistent or recurrent physical or psychological problems that are likely to be caused or exacerbated by alcohol (DSM-IV, p. 181). Thus, control and/or manageability are seriously impaired.

Alcohol abuse describes a maladaptive pattern of alcohol use that leads to significant distress as manifested by one or more of the following occurring within a twelve month period: (1) Recurrent alcohol use results in a failure to fulfill major roles obligatory at work, school, home, etc. (2) Alcohol is used in situations in which it is physically hazardous (e.g., driving). (3) Legal problems result from alcohol use. (4) Drinking continues despite undergoing persistent or recurrent social or interpersonal problems caused by or exacerbated by alcohol (e.g., arguments). (5) Finally, the criteria for alcohol dependence has never been met (DSM-IV, pp. 182-183, 196).

In short, the primary difference between alcohol dependence and abuse is that abuse does not include tolerance, withdrawal, or a pattern of compulsive use. Instead, abuse focuses on the harmful consequences of repeated use (DSM-IV, p. 182).

DSM-IV also describes "alcohol-induced disorders" — disorders that are caused or exacerbated by alcohol and are distinct from, but may be associated with, alcohol dependence or abuse. For instance, alcohol intoxication and alcohol withdrawal are often results of alcohol dependence, but they may be a once-in-a-lifetime experience. Other alcohol-induced disorders include sleep disorders, sexual dysfunctions, mental disorders, and mood and anxiety disorders (DSM-IV, pp. 196-199).

For our purpose, normal alcoholics do not usually meet the criteria for alcohol dependence, for they seldom manifest dysfunctional behavior like a blatant lack of control, difficulty in meeting one's responsibilities, giving up important activities, and increased tolerance and withdrawal. However, alcohol abuse describes normal alcoholics in that they continue to drink despite problems to self and others and yet function well in comparison to others and without symptoms of psychological dependence. "Abusive drinking," although commonly tolerated and sanctioned, is alcoholic. Along with this psychiatric approach, let us consider some other psychological models that can also contribute to our understanding of alcoholism.

Psychological Models

Unlike the preceding models, most psychological models do not offer a specific theory of alcoholism, but rather they offer general theories of how and why people think, feel, and behave. Nevertheless, these general approaches can be used to understand and treat alcoholism. At the risk of being simplistic our intent is to show how different psychological perspectives might construe alcoholism.

From a Freudian perspective, one way to understand alcoholism is as a symptom of arrested development, particularly oral fixation. For instance, normal alcoholics cope with problems via drinking because they learned that oral gratification evokes comfort and safety — that is, "makes everything all right." When uncomfortable, they regress to oral gratification. Thus, to achieve sobriety, alcoholics need to work through their oral fixation and learn healthy ways to manage their anxiety. They learn to replace their dependence on the bottle with more rational and effective coping. Such strengthening of ego functions is a common goal in rehabilitation programs as well as in individual therapy.

Looking through the prism of Client-centered or Rogerian theory, alcoholism can be seen as a maladaptive way to lessen the discomfort of unacceptable feelings. Successful counseling would include no longer needing to drink to numb, distort, or deny unacceptable experiences or to fulfill conditions (drinking) of worth. With unconditional acceptance, understanding, and positive regard, client-centered counselors would encourage alcoholics to express and accept their feelings (affect) so they can learn to be in harmony with and feel better about themselves.

Drug treatment programs usually include affective approaches such as client-centered and Gestalt therapies that focus on sharing and becoming aware of feelings. By means of reflective listening in individual and group settings, role playing, and experiential exercises, alcoholics learn to admit and manage their feelings in more adaptable and acceptable ways than drinking. Self-esteem usually improves as well as self-congruence or serenity.

Cognitive approaches basically state that our cognition (attitudes, beliefs, expectations) determine the way we act (behavior) and feel (affect). Consequently, a goal in cognitive therapy is to change the way we think about drinking and follow thoughts that foster sober living. For example, some men may unknowingly hold the belief that being a man is to be a heavy drinker or that having fun must include drinking. Or rather than deceiving themselves with false beliefs and promises ("I'm in control," "Drinking won't hurt me," "I deserve it"), or as A.A. would say with "stinkin' thinkin'," alcoholics can stop/change negative thoughts and learn to follow positive thinking.

For instance, following the belief that you have a disease is probably more effective than believing you are a "bad person." A disease (of alcoholism) is curable, limited, and impersonal and it minimizes guilt, shame, and low self-esteem. In contrast, bad character is more permanent, pervasive, and personal as well as maximizing guilt, shame, and low self-esteem. A cognitive psychologist would argue that believing you are bad because you drink engenders helplessness, hopelessness, and self-hate. On the other hand, construing alcoholism as a disease engenders action or seeking a cure as well as renewing hope and self-worth. Thus your thinking highly influences how responsible and forward looking you are — or, how likely you are to change for the better.

Many A.A. slogans can be construed as "cognitive restructuring." For example, recovering people are encouraged to follow certain principles and to repeat slogans like "Fake it to make it," "Easy does it," "One day at a time," "Let go, let God," "Think," in spite of and often contrary to the way they feel. By trusting and practicing the thinking of others, they eventually implement such thinking in behavior and begin to feel better. Instead of following their feelings to drink, they practice sober thinking and behaving.

Instead of cognition, learning/theories focus primarily on

behavior. Putting on the glasses of "operant conditioning," we can look at drinking alcoholically as behavior that satisfies needs which reinforces drinking behavior. Thus, the reward of "contented" feelings increases the likelihood of drinking. To extinguish the "stimulus-response pattern" of alcoholism, alcoholics stop reinforcing the drinking behavior and learn to manage the remaining tension. Alcoholics can learn to tolerate short-term discomfort in service of long-term sobriety. And eventually, the rewards of sobriety reinforce sober living.

To "desensitize" drinking behavior, alcoholics can also learn relaxation procedures to reduce anxiety when they feel the urge to drink. Such relaxation reduces anxiety as well as reinforces sober living. Furthermore, alcoholics can give themselves or receive rewards for not drinking. In many A.A. meetings, for instance, recovering alcoholics are given social and often material recognition (e.g., applause, hugs, anniversary cake, medallion) for achieving a sobriety date, which serve as positive reinforcements of sobriety.

According to Miller and Dollard's learning theory, alcoholism can be considered a learned negative habit that can be broken or weakened by the absence of reward. Simply stated, the desire to drink cannot be reinforced by the behavior of drinking. To extinguish the habit of alcoholism it is important to control the cues that elicit and guide the alcoholic response. For instance, such cues as alcoholic friends, places, and events as well as more subtle internal cues like alcoholic thinking, day dreaming, or reminiscing can be avoided. Cues are like temptations that provoke the need to drink and that lure alcoholics to drink. Although habits are difficult to change, controlling the variables increases the likelihood of achieving change.

Another form of learning theory is "classical conditioning," which basically means that a neutral stimulus can evoke a new response by pairing the neutral stimulus with another stimulus. For example, the stimulus of a newspaper may evoke no response from a dog, but when it is paired with anger and discomfort (swatting the dog), it elicits a response (fear) from the dog. Likewise, neutral objects or stimuli such as glasses, bottles, and parties when paired with drinking can evoke pleasant alcoholic times. For instance, if you give water in a beer mug to a non alcoholic, the person simply drinks the water. But if you give the same mug to an alcoholic (beer) drinker, it may evoke an entirely different response. Thus, it behooves an alcoholic to abstain from objects (stimuli) that are associated with and evoke the habitual desire and response to drink.

Still another learning approach is "social learning" theory, which basically states that we learn behavior through observation. Simply put, what we see is what we learn. Learning through observation or modeling is especially important because of the enormous input of mass media. Besides being bombarded by questionable models that are often ageist, sexist, and racist, media advertisements and commercials pressure viewers to drink to feel good (operant conditioning) and associate (classical conditioning) drugs with being successful, happy, or even being a "true" man or woman (social learning).

Parents and other significant people also serve as models so that children are likely to learn from what they observe more than from what they are told. "Do what I say, not what I do" simply does not work. To tell a child not to drink while drinking can engender ambiguous and ambivalent feelings. In fact, we can punish our children for doing what we teach them to do; thus they learn to drink and feel guilty about it.

Learning through observation also forms our expectations which influence our behavior. For instance, we can learn through passive and unconscious observation that drinking alcohol promises fun so that we expect to have fun while drinking and perhaps a boring time when not drinking. To extinguish drinking patterns, we have to control what we observe as well as be aware of our expectations.

Conversely, we can expose ourselves to healthy, sober models that positively influence our own sobriety. For instance, lead speakers at A.A. meetings, sponsors, other sober persons, and A.A. as a whole are examples of healthy and effective modeling. Unfortunately, few normal alcoholics give witness to their recovery and continued sobriety.

Although we may not be able to state conclusively that the operant, classical, S-R (Stimulus-Response) habit formation, or social learning approaches cause alcoholism, we can say that such learning can significantly influence our drinking patterns. Thus, it behooves us to be aware of and manage the factors that evoke, increase the likelihood of, or reinforce alcoholic responses as well as drives, stimuli, cues, behavior, media and environmental models that induce and form alcoholic drinking.

Moral Models

Before the advent of medical and psychological models, moral models were the primary means of dealing with alcoholism. Rather than taking a disease entity or psychological approach, alcoholism was and often is judged in terms of its "goodness" and "badness."

Moral systems vary on a broad continuum from professional (religious, theological) to personal (moderate, liberal, conservative). For instance, some people see alcoholism as a serious sin, or an imperfection. Some religions forbid drinking, while others incorporate alcohol in their rituals. Few if any moral or religious systems encourage alcoholism. Since our personalized system — what we think and do when we confront alcohol, its use and/or abuse — is the critical factor in how we treat alcoholics, it behooves us to be aware of the moral theories we use in making our judgments.

Underlying some of our models of morality is the assumption that people choose and learn to be alcoholic or sober. Unlike an impersonal disease which one does not choose, alcoholism is more like a vice or sin which is a result of bad choices or bad character. Assuming that alcoholism can be stopped with willpower, it follows that excessive drinking is sinful or at least a moral weakness. Statements like the following ones indicate such a moral approach: "If you cared, you would stop drinking." "You purposely drink to hurt me." "Some day you'll go to hell for drinking." "If I really wanted to stop, I would." "Why am I so bad?"

Some focus on the subjectivity of the alcoholic and argue that the morality of alcoholism depends on many factors such as one's degree of maturity, responsibility, and freedom as well as situational factors. People who subscribe to the disease model are apt to consider alcoholism as an amoral issue because alcoholism is a disease rather than a sin. Others argue that alcoholics are not morally culpable for their condition, but they are morally responsible for their recovery.

Others would argue that alcoholism fails to fit the definition of a disease and is consequently an irresponsible way to construe alcoholism. They contend that such a model induces helplessness and excludes moral culpability and responsibility. Like other transgressions (stealing, lying, adultery, etc.), alcoholism is a choice, not a disease.

Indeed, there are various views. A key question is what is your moral view toward alcoholism? Is alcoholism a moral or amoral issue? If so, then how and why? Is alcoholism a choice? Is it immoral for an alcoholic to continue drinking without trying to achieve sobriety? Does alcoholism, of whatever type, impede a good/spiritual life? Can you be an active alcoholic saint?

Systems Theory

Systems theory is a common approach in inpatient and outpatient treatment programs as well as in after-care and relapse prevention programs. Furthermore, it is used not only with alcoholics but also with co- and para-alcoholics — people who are involved with and influenced by alcoholics. Systems theory basically states that since people are all integral members of a system such as a family, neighborhood, or any kind of community, they interact with and influence one another. Consequently, the way one person behaves highly impacts others.

For instance, when one member of a family becomes dysfunctional or alcoholic, the other members are influenced and are pressured to cope in dysfunctional ways, like denying, enabling, and entering collusion. Such coping expends considerable energy as well as causing an enormous amount of stress and more negative coping. To survive and maintain the system, people learn to play dysfunctional roles such as the caretaker, martyr, clown, aggressor or scapegoat. The rules often include collusive denial and not feeling, trusting, and speaking truth. In this way, alcoholism is maintained as a family disease.

A way to regain healthy balance in the family or any system is to break through denial, accept what is really going on, and learn to cope and interact in healthier ways. For instance, when co-dependents learn to function effectively, they stop being overly responsible and enabling and start influencing the alcoholic positively. Programs for co-dependents such as Al-Anon, Al-Ateen, Co-Dependents Anonymous, POTADA, and Adult Children of Alcoholics (ACoA) emphasize taking responsibility to change one's self. Paradoxically, the paramount way to help others is to help oneself.

Consider co-alcoholics (co-dependents) in light of twelve step and systems approaches. Co-alcoholics accept that they are powerless over the alcoholic's alcoholism, but with the help of God and others, they can learn to manage effectively as well as live serenely. They learn to detach themselves from the alcoholic's behavior while loving the alcoholic. They learn to avoid unnecessary guilt, to let go of resentment, to increase self-esteem, and to take care of themselves. And becoming healthy, they encourage other members of the alcoholic system, including the alcoholic, to strive for sobriety.

A systems approach can also help alcoholics to realize how

their alcoholic behavior negatively influences others. As one alcoholic said: "When I am tempted to drink or even talk about taking a drink, I can see the intense fear in my family members. If for no other reason, I wouldn't drink because of the pain it causes them." Furthermore, recovering alcoholics also invite and spontaneously pressure people to grow. In short, when one member — alcoholic, co-alcoholic, adult child — becomes sober, other people are encouraged to improve.

So after reflecting on these theories, how do you construe alcoholism? What model do you really follow? Remember: Your personal view strongly influences the way you judge, feel about, and cope with alcoholics. Our next project is to use these models to formulate an integrative model of normal alcoholism.

3 Normal Alcoholism

To challenge and improve our personal theories, we have presented various professional ways to construe and treat alcoholism. A primary thesis has been that our personal and professional theories highly influence the way we cope with and treat alcoholics.

A major concern is that normal alcoholics are not recognized as often as alcoholics who have a primary, chronic, progressive and fatal disease and whose life has become unmanageable. Normal alcoholics usually manage relatively better and experience less debilitating effects. Thus, they are more functional, and they may avoid therapeutic programs like A.A.

Arguably, such alcoholics may be in denial, deluding themselves with the illusion of control or "terminal uniqueness" — and this criticism may be true. Indeed, many so-called normal alcoholics progress to more abnormal alcoholism. Furthermore, so-called normal alcoholics are alcoholics and therefore are far more similar to than different from other alcoholics. All alcoholics are on the same boat, albeit in different sections, "nourishing" themselves with the same spirits. It is as if normal alcoholics can sail on the alcoholic boat longer and more functionally than some other alcoholics. Nevertheless, all alcoholics suffer unnecessarily and miss too much on their "voyage." There are better ways to travel.

In short, various kinds of alcoholisms or alcoholics partake of and manifest the same reality of alcoholism. To move toward achieving a unity of understanding and treatment, a general theory of alcoholism is needed to incorporate what is common to all forms of alcoholism. On this basis, a specific theory of normal alcoholism will be offered.

A General Theory of Alcoholism

Consider alcoholism as *an obsessive concern about and a compulsive use of alcohol that produces desired effects as well as negative consequences*. Reflect on the four parts of this definition.

First, alcoholics are more or less obsessed with thoughts of drinking that manifest themselves in idle thinking, dreams, fantasies, intrusive thoughts, and concrete plans. Jan explains her addictive thinking in this way: "It's not as if I always thought of drinking and couldn't concentrate on my work. Actually, I was an excellent accountant and advanced quickly. But I really looked forward to drinking after work. It was as if drinking was my reward for a job well done; it motivated me. Weekends and holidays were bonuses because I didn't have to be so careful about drinking too much. Again, I looked forward to these good times; a weekend without them felt unfair, empty, and scary. I felt when life was difficult, I could think of better times to come.

Alcoholics look forward to drinking, think about and give reasons for not drinking, justify their drinking, lie about and hide their drinking, or think about the comfort of drinking. When drinking is one's primary concern, all thinking is more or less colored by and eventually in the service of drinking. Simply stated: A lot of thought is given to drinking. Furthermore, like Jan, the promise of drinking in the near future helps alcoholics to relax in the present, and conversely the thought of not being able to drink for an indefinite time evokes anxiety and subtle sadness. Non-alcoholics simply do not think this way; such thoughts, fantasies, and feelings neither exist nor demand attention.

Second, alcoholics feel more or less compelled to use alcohol as a means of effecting changes in mood, thinking, or overall well-being. They feel a desire that drives them to use alcohol — to achieve contentment, to effect a "buzz," to reduce tension, to numb feelings, to "feel freer," to forget, to relax, to reward and nourish themselves, to feel better. And, their pleasant feelings reinforce the compulsion to use again.

Why are some people compelled to drink alcoholically, while others are not? No one knows for sure. As we have seen, there are many ways to explain alcoholism. Some approaches accent organic/genetic/biochemical factors, others emphasize non-organic/psychogenic/environmental factors, and others try to integrate both nature and nurture. Depending on the person, there can be many reasons (and combinations thereof) to feel compelled to drink — such as genetics, biochemistry, habit, stress mismanagement, expectations, environmental pressure, cultural and societal sanctions, etc.

One drink can compel some alcoholics to drink until they pass out or get sick. For them, one drink is too many. Other alcoholics feel compelled to drink daily while managing to function without blatant disruption. Others feel compelled to drink only on weekends, during holidays, or at festive occasions. Others seldom drink, but when they do, they drink alcoholically.

Like Jan, many alcoholics feel that they are entitled to drink and that life without alcohol is somehow not right, incomplete, or difficult. Although most alcoholics can abstain from drinking (be dry), they miss it. Their efforts to abstain, which include intense willpower (white knuckle approach), making "great sacrifices," irritability, constant complaints or bragging, or "dry drunks," give evidence of their compulsion.

Listen to a Lenten abstainer: "Every Lent I would go on the wagon and people would applaud me for my self-control and sacrifice. Certainly, my Lenten abstinence was proof positive that I was not an alcoholic. Ah! What deception! And, everyone including myself believed. To reinforce my Lenten deception, I would periodically quit drinking for several months to lose weight. Interestingly, I never quit during the holidays, but usually after. And I knew that I could return to drinking, which seemed to ease the tension. And besides, I did lose weight. It was as if my urge to drink was put on hold, but I knew that it was always there to return to. To quit forever was untenable and frightening."

The third part of this description refers to the reasons for drinking alcoholically. Alcoholics seldom drink to feel miserable; on the contrary, they drink to feel "better" — "free," high, buzzed, mellow, and content rather than tense, confined, low, conflicted, harsh, and discontent. And such "gains," payoffs, or rewards reinforce drinking so that the likelihood of drinking again is increased.

Another of alcoholism's powerful dynamics, which reinforces its obsessiveness and compulsiveness, is the relative certainty and immediacy of its rewards. Unlike the risk and uncertainty of interpersonal fulfillment, alcoholics can safely count on the effects of drinking. Drinking seldom lets them down; it usually gives them what they ask for.

Alcoholic effects are easy to come by and occur quickly. There is little waiting; the rewards are immediate. Compounding the certainty and immediacy of gratification is the easy availability of alcohol. Alcohol is legal and easily acquired. As one alcoholic said, "Why wait for the harvest of sobriety when the fruits of alcohol are ready at hand?"

"My two to four double martinis after work was a ritual for me," explains Tom. "Without them, I felt cheated — like a reward that I earned was not given to me. Besides, it was easy. The booze was there and nobody seriously hassled me. I could depend on getting pleasantly mellow before dinner, and on maintaining the feeling of coasting on air with one or two more drinks after dinner. Although I was usually polite and solicitous, I'm sorry to say that my family was off in the distance and secondary to my primary concern of drinking. I eventually fell asleep around 10:00 o'clock, and around 12:30 I awakened and went to bed. My routine was apparently harmless, easy, dependable, safe, private, effortless, and pleasant. And the negative effects? Well, I thought, I might die before they come."

Fourth, there are immediate and long term negative consequences of drinking alcoholically. With the severe and relatively dysfunctional (gamma, dependent) alcoholic, the consequences are usually obvious. Some alcoholics may undergo personality changes that are blatantly destructive such as violent arguing, physical aggression, drunken binges, and severe hangovers. Such immediate consequences make life unmanageable and are usually followed by other consequences like loss of friends, family, and job as well as legal difficulties and perhaps institutionalization.

In contrast, normal alcoholics usually manage their drinking within socially acceptable norms, i.e., their drinking seldom gets out of hand to the extent of embarrassment or of being seriously disruptive. And they usually function well, particularly at work. Their consequences are more private and easier to deny, rationalize, and manage.

Some alcoholics, like gamma alcoholics, experience blatant physical, psychosocial, and spiritual harm to self and others. Beta alcoholics also have little control insofar as drinking causes medical problems and often consequent psychosocial problems. Likewise, the APA's diagnosis of alcohol dependency includes obvious negative consequences — loss of control, withdrawal symptoms upon abstinence, progressive drinking, increased tolerance and chronicity and effects from tissue and metabolic changes.

However, as Jellinek points out, not all alcoholics lose control, and similar to the APA DSM-IV it is possible to be an alcohol abuser who does not suffer withdrawal symptoms and who may have considerable control over abusive drinking. Normal alcoholics manage significantly better than chronic gamma or dependent type alcoholics. Nevertheless, as we have indicated, normal alcoholics are also obsessed with, feel compelled to use, experience "positive" effects, and undergo negative consequences.

Alcoholism: A Way of Being

Reflecting on this phenomenology of alcoholism, we can see that alcoholism is construed as "a way of being." Alcoholism is not only an illness that you have but also an orientation to reality — a mode of being or living. Thus, it is not so much a matter of "how much" you drink but more a matter of "how" and "why" you drink.

Construing alcoholism primarily as a dis-eased way of being includes all types of alcoholism — from normal to abnormal, from mild to moderate to severe, from alpha/abuser to gamma/dependent. All alcoholics share common characteristics while allowing for many individual differences. Sooner or later, all alcoholics turn to alcohol for comfort, peace, relief, fun, freedom. In practice, alcohol is their ultimate concern and saving grace. In this sense, alcoholism can be seen as a displacement of God — or a Higher Power.

Since alcohol is one's core motivating force in life, everything and everyone is influenced by and eventually in the service of alcohol. Alcoholics see with alcoholic eyes: alcohol permeates their perception of reality. Sensation, cognition, volition, affectivity, memory, values, and behavior are more or less influenced by alcoholism. Too often, alcohol is significant in experiencing the worth of a situation. Life without alcohol is experienced as disconcerting and lacking. In short, the worlds of alcoholism are similar to and differ from the worlds of sobriety. Their ways of being are similar and different.

A distinction can be made between "being an alcoholic" and "being alcoholic." Some alcoholics feel more comfortable describing themselves as "alcoholic" rather than identifying themselves as "an alcoholic." When we say: "I am an alcoholic," we affirm and admit to the reality of being an alcoholic, decrease the possibilities of deceiving ourselves, and increase the likelihood of following a program of recovery. A danger, however, is to categorize oneself and others — to identify oneself as an alcoholic and consequently minimize other modes of being. Indeed, although one may be an alcoholic, he or she is infinitely more than an alcoholic.

"Alcoholic" can also be used as an adjective so that instead of saying that "I am an alcoholic," we can say, "I am alcoholic." Keeping in mind that language influences our experience of reality, to admit being alcoholic may be helpful especially in the initial stages of acceptance and recovery. Many people identify "an alcoholic" with being a derelict, a disruptive and out of control drinker, or at least an irresponsible person — with someone totally "other" than they themselves or loved ones are. Thus, to admit to "drinking alcoholically" may be more acceptable. Saying that I am an alcoholic may also evoke treatment programs, A.A., or changes which threaten, embarrass, and shame some alcoholics. So if it is helpful, feel free to say: "I am alcoholic." Eventually, alcoholics come to realize that there are many alcoholisms/alcoholics — ways of being an alcoholic and of being alcoholic. In our framework, "alcoholic" is used as both a noun and an adjective — "being alcoholic" and being "an alcoholic." Both are modes of being.

Listen to this normal alcoholic. "When I first started to go to A.A. meetings, I liked the program and found it helpful, but I didn't feel part of the fellowship. Something was missing. I can recall a discussion meeting on the first three steps where I expressed some doubt about being an alcoholic, and one of the members shot back: 'If it looks like a duck, walks like a duck, and quacks like a duck, then it is a duck.' Theoretically, I knew what he meant, but I felt misunderstood and alienated. To extend the metaphor, I didn't look, walk, or talk like most of the ducks in A.A., yet I did look, walk, and talk in ways that were alcoholic.

"Weeks later I shared this experience with my sponsor, who said that I didn't have to say that I am an alcoholic. She reminded me that the only A.A. requirement is a desire to stop drinking. She suggested that since I drank alcoholically, that perhaps I could say that I am alcoholic rather than being 'an alcoholic.' I felt understood; somehow this made more sense. Now I can say that I am an alcoholic, reminding myself that I don't have to be the same kind of duck as others. And I am a member of the fellowship. This duck finally feels at home."

To conclude: Normal alcoholics would include alpha, delta, and alcohol abuser types of alcoholism. The gamma, beta, and substance dependent alcoholics would be relatively less normal and controlled (more powerless) and have more difficulty managing than more normal alcoholics. (Epsilon alcoholics move between the extremes of controlled abstinence and powerless drinking.) Thus, instead of discussing "alcoholism," it is appropriate to speak of "alcoholisms." Thus, while all alcoholics are different, they share a way of being.

A Continuum of Drinking

Consider alcoholism on a continuum as a helpful way to reflect on the healthiness/non-healthiness/unhealthiness of alcohol consumption. Such a continuum begins with healthy abstinence that can move to normal-healthy (infrequent drinking with neither obsessive-compulsive components nor negative consequences) and abnormal-unhealthy (obsessive-compulsive patterns, powerlessness, unmanageableness, and blatant negative consequences) drinking. In this sense, normal alcoholism is neither healthy nor unhealthy but rather normal yet alcoholic. Let me explain this apparent contradiction.

Many alcoholics are "normal" insofar as they can satisfy basic needs, manage to cope effectively, and are reasonably successful. They keep societal norms, are socially acceptable and sometimes are admired. Rarely are they labeled abnormal, unhealthy, or alcoholic. In short, they are mostly like everyone else — normal.

Nevertheless, these alcoholics are alcoholic insofar as their drinking impedes, often subtly, fuller and freer living. Unlike

abnormal alcoholism which revolves around serious dysfunctionality and social unacceptability, normal alcoholism usually
involves impediments to intimacy and/or one's spiritual life. In
short, many alcoholics are both normal (psychologically functional and acceptable) and "mad" (less than whole): "normally
mad," or normal and alcoholic.

In contrast, some alcoholics have difficulty managing and
coping with everyday demands, become progressively offensive
to self and others, fail to follow or violate accepted norms, and
tend to conflict with what is normal. Their abnormality is manifested in overt negative consequences such as destruction of family relationships, loss of job, legal problems, interpersonal violence, and other personal damage to themselves and others. These
alcoholics tend to stand out to objective observers who are not
in denial or collusion.

Thus, alcoholism (of whatever type) is less than healthy.
Some alcoholics are more normal than abnormal in regard to
their psychological and social functioning while others are more
abnormal than normal. Both normal (functional) and abnormal
(less functional), alcoholisms are mad or non-healthy, i.e., less
than healthy or whole.

Normal alcoholics behave well in task-oriented, social, legal, and economic situations. They are not judged to be "unhealthy" and/or abnormal because they function well and are
socially accepted; nevertheless, they are not healthy. In short,
normal alcoholics are neither healthy (whole) nor unhealthy
(pathologically dysfunctional); they are normal and alcoholic
(mad).

To be sure, both normal and abnormal alcoholics are alcoholic, persons who are obsessed with and compelled to use alcohol. Alcohol plays too much of a role in their ways of being. The
diagnosis is based on the differences in severity and degree of
unmanageableness, lack of wholeness, and negative consequences
to self and others.

Although normal alcoholics usually manage well with task-oriented reality, they do not relate as well with non task-oriented experiences, like intimacy. Such alpha, delta, or alcohol abusers perform well on the front stage of life, but their back stage behavior is more problematic. In contrast, the front stage (public) behavior of gamma/dependent alcoholics is more disruptive, for they cannot function as consistently or as well as more functional alcoholics.

In contrast to normal-abnormal alcoholics, healthy-normal drinkers are not obsessed about alcohol; in fact, they rarely if ever think about drinking. Nor do they feel compelled to use. Rather, drinking may be part of a ritual, social gathering, or a dinner that flows naturally from other activities. Their drinking adds to an already good time. Alcohol is low on their priority list; they can take it or leave it without feeling deprived. Their way of being is not alcoholic.

Seldom, if ever, do healthy drinkers drink too much, and when they do, they quickly forget about it and do not soon desire to drink again. Although healthy drinkers may occasionally talk and even joke about drinking, they neither obsess about nor urgently desire it. Alcohol simply does not play an important role in their life. In contrast, alcoholics of whatever kind obsess about and feel urged to repeat the alcoholic experiences. They take drinking very seriously.

Looking at alcoholism from a continuum perspective, many kinds of drinkers can be described. Some healthy drinkers never progress to alcoholism, and others do. Some people become normal-functional alcoholics who never become blatantly dysfunctional, while others sooner or later become progressively abnormal-dysfunctional. Fast progression from normal experimentation with alcohol (and/or other drugs) to functional abuse and onto dysfunctional addiction is particularly true with young adolescents who are predisposed to alcoholism. In contrast, people who begin to drink later in life may become normal alcoholics for many years or even decades and slowly progress into less manageable alcoholism. And, there are many people who never drink at all.

Our challenge is to be aware of when normal healthy drinking begins to lead to normal alcoholism and possibly progress to abnormal alcoholism. Ideally we should intervene early in the progression of alcoholism. Keep in mind that most unmanageable alcoholics once managed well. Metaphorically or literally, the "skid-row bum" may have once been a community model.

Our concern is normal alcoholism — with people who are between healthy drinking and unhealthy alcoholism. And, since normal alcoholics are in the middle of the continuum — being more normal (manageable) than abnormal (unmanageable), they can easily go unrecognized and untreated.

A Specific Theory of Normal Alcoholism

We have seen that normal alcoholism simply means that a person is both normal and alcoholic. From a psychosocial perspective, alcoholics are normal when they can satisfy needs, manage effectively, cope with life's demands, communicate, work, behave within societal norms, and achieve success. But, they drink alcoholically because they are obsessed with and compelled to use alcohol and because their negative consequences are greater than their so-called positive ones. Although they are more normal ("like us") than abnormal ("like them"), they are not healthy.

Since normal alcoholics do well, it is difficult for them to stop drinking. They maintain their lifestyles, function relatively and often quite well, are sane insofar as they are seldom judged insane, are self-sufficient, and they exercise control and choice. Particularly when they are not concerned about the impact they make on others, normal alcoholics can easily deceive themselves. Such is their brand of insanity.

Their acceptable and functional behavior hides and minimizes the negative consequences. For example, many alcoholics are successful in their work, which tends to cover negative consequences in their more personal and interpersonal lives. Since the measure of our worth is frequently based on what we functionally do and have rather than on who and what we are, it is understandable that we can easily rationalize, deny, or misdiagnose the more normal modes of alcoholism.

Listen to Joan, the wife of a recovering alcoholic. "For the first twenty years of our marriage, I never thought Jay was alcoholic. Not until the kids were on their own and Jay and I had to face each other did I begin to wonder. After several years of tension and doubt, I joined Al-Anon and began to admit what was really going on, including my enabling role.

"It is understandable that I denied Jay's alcoholism and rationalized that he simply liked to drink and deserved to relax. Look, not only did he never miss work but he became a senior vice-president. Furthermore, he always did chores around the house, was thoughtful, took the kids places, went to church. He never got in trouble; in fact, he helped people in trouble. Compared to other men, he was a good husband and father. So why do I think he was an alcoholic?

"Although Jay did his duty and was a good man, he is a better man since he stopped drinking and became sober. Now, I feel that he is more in touch — that he listens to me more consistently and with interest. He's simply more present. In the past, he would half listen and not be fully interested in what I had to say. And on weekends he would disappear to the den to work or watch television and drink.

"Since he is sober, I feel that Jay is much more honest and he avoids less and shares more. And although love making was always passionate, I feel we now share more genuinely. I used to feel that he was not quite there for me. Now I feel he is really with me. And I feel I am number one, not second to booze."

Listen to Jay. "It's not so much what I did when I was drinking, but more what I didn't do. I functioned well — being more successful than anyone we know. I managed my drinking so that it would not impede my career. For instance, most of my drinking was done at home, and I was sure to stop in time so that I could manage well the next day. But now that I'm sober, I work even better and overall I have more energy.

"One difference is I don't have to use time and energy to hide my drinking and myself. Actually, there is nothing much, if anything, to hide. In the past I felt I was a perpetual juggler always manipulating life so that I could go to my source of happiness — booze. Now, I have healthier sources of nourishment and happiness. I feel freer and cleaner, more worthwhile, more energy, more alive. I feel better about myself.

"I can go on and on. For instance, good times seem to linger longer and more vividly, and I can remember and enjoy them. In fact, it never ceases to amaze me that I can do even more than I used to. My spiritual life is also better. I always was moral and religious, but now I am really developing a personal relationship with God that makes all the difference in the world.

"Day by day, I feel stronger, freer, more worthwhile. I feel I really face my wife and kids — reality, better. It's like I see better, and therefore can deal with and enjoy life better. Better! I guess that's the word."

Any alcoholism results in immediate and long term negative consequences. Consequences of normal alcoholism are usually more manageable, subtle, tolerated, and easily minimized as well as less blatantly destructive than those of more dysfunctional (gamma/dependent) alcoholisms. Nevertheless, all alcoholic consequences do serious harm. To paraphrase one of Jellinek's definitions: Alcoholics, whatever type or degree, drink in such a way that the negative consequences to self and others are greater than the positive consequences.

The word addiction, coming from the Latin *ad-dicere*, literally means "to speak to." Being alcoholic means to speak to and listen to alcohol far too much and far too often. Alcohol simply means too much. Are normal alcoholics addicts? Yes and no. Yes, insofar as they obsess and feel urged to drink. Alcohol simply plays a primary and central role rather than a secondary and peripheral role. Unlike the healthy drinker, alcohol frequently beckons the normal alcoholic to become involved with it.

Normal alcoholics are not addicts in that they are not gamma or dependent alcoholics who manage poorly, nor are they likely to have serious physical withdrawal symptoms. Addicted alcoholics have an explicit and sloppy love affair with alcohol that is often and obviously disruptive; whereas normal alcoholics have a more subtle, silent, smoother, and sneaky love affair. Both are affairs.

Normal alcoholics may or may not progress in their dis-ease. Those who do progress, usually over many years and often decades, become less functional, regress into unmanageableness, become powerless, and manifest more explicit and dysfunctional symptoms. Others, who do not progress as much or as blatantly, tend to maintain themselves, or they slowly and silently dissipate.

The slow progression often has periods of abstinence. For instance, "religious alcoholics" may quit during Lent, abstaining from alcohol for six and a half weeks, only to drink excessively on Easter Sunday or soon after. Some alcoholics abstain months or years at a time only to return to drinking alcoholically. Once again because of such periods of abstinence and its relatively subtle negative consequences, normal alcoholics can easily deceive themselves and others.

Although normal alcoholics may live good and successful lives, let us not canonize or enter into collusion with them. Particularly when drinking, their behavior and language betray a certain self-centeredness and self will. Whether aggressive, withdrawn, or pleasing, they do get what they want — alcohol. Like other addicts, normal alcoholics chase the high, want to feel better, seek serenity, and desire immediate fulfillment.

Degrees of Normal Alcoholism

Another way of looking at normal alcoholism is to differ-
entiate degrees, namely: from mild to moderate to severe. Mild
alcoholics, for instance, meet their responsibilities, can usually
be depended upon, function well, and are seen by others as being quite normal. Nevertheless, they use alcohol somewhat obsessively and compulsively, too often to cope with stressful situations and uncomfortable feelings.

Jane, a 38-year-old homemaker with two preteen sons and
two teenage daughters, has been drinking for the past ten years,
since her youngest son started school. She had dedicated her life
to being a super mother and wife — always ready to serve and
help her children and husband as well as do considerable volunteer work. However, when her boys are in bed and her girls are
out late or overnight, she drinks. She has one or two stiff scotch
and sodas, watches television while drinking, and eventually falls
asleep. (Realize that women need significantly less alcohol to alter
themselves.) The next morning she takes an aspirin for her slight
hangover and functions well.

However, Jane's marriage is not very healthy. Although she
and her husband seldom argue, neither are they intimate nor do
they have much fun together. Her husband is a classic workaholic
who rarely drinks but is seldom at home. In fact, Jane often won-
ders if he is having an affair. But instead of listening to her feelings, Jane numbs them with alcohol and drifts off into her own
fantasy world.

How long Jane can continue to live this lifestyle is a question that will be answered in the future. Presently her kids love
her, and her workaholic husband seems satisfied. Perhaps once
her children leave home and she is alone with her husband, she
may progress to moderate and even to severe alcoholism. Or she
may face her crisis and learn to cope and live soberly. One never
knows for sure what will happen.

"Moderately" normal alcoholics also function well and meet

their social, work, and family responsibilities, but they tend to obsess more about alcohol and often drink more compulsively than mild alcoholics. For instance, they may not drink much during the week, but at social gatherings, on weekends, and on vacations their drinking escalates significantly.

Some abstain from alcohol for months and then resume daily moderate drinking. Some abstain during the week, but on weekends drink moderately to the extent that they fall asleep. They rarely if ever become explicitly drunk, but their mood, visual-motor coordination, thinking, speech, and decision making are not up to sober par.

Again, most people would not identify such persons as alcoholic, but more likely as persons who work hard and relax via drinking. Publicly, moderately functional alcoholics may be a lot of fun, but privately their drinking causes family problems and particularly problems of intimacy.

"I knew something was wrong, but I felt guilty if I complained." "You see," says this 49-year-old homemaker, "my husband did everything I asked him to do; so, how could I complain? Anyhow, I don't like to complain. Still, it's not what he did, but sort of how he wasn't. Let me try to explain.

"I often had the feeling that Greg was not quite there — there for me. Especially when we were alone with each other, I felt as though he were half with me, as if he were half someplace else. I knew Greg drank too much, but he was always pleasant. Yes, he would often fall asleep early; at least I could see that. It was when he was asleep and awake at the same time that it was frustrating.

"Now that Greg is sober for five years, I can feel the difference. Greg is simply more present to me. He is more alert, more consistent, more feeling, more touchable — more. Although it's still elusive, the difference makes a huge difference. Greg is more Greg. Since he has removed his mask, we can come face to face."

Severe or barely normal alcoholics are on the verge of or are becoming gamma or dependent alcoholics. They may be the persons who cannot wait to get home to have a couple of drinks. Or they may have a two martini lunch, have a couple more drinks after work, and after dinner have a few more. They live for feeling better through alcohol. Although such persons often function in a fog, they are able to function well enough to be as professionally successful as many or most of their peers.

These alcoholics are on the brink of losing control. Despite managing to cope, their life is beginning to become unmanageable. Although others are apt to see them as having a drinking problem, they are not likely to judge them as alcoholic. Actually these alcoholics are sometimes admired for being successful heavy drinkers. Although they may not be diagnosed as alcohol dependent (gamma alcoholic) or addicted, they do abuse alcohol (alpha alcoholic). To call them less than alcoholics is doing them a disservice.

Hitting Bottom

Still another way to shed light on normal alcoholism is to discuss "hitting bottom." "Hitting bottom" and "bottoming out" are popular expressions in drug and alcoholic treatment programs. Hitting bottom occurs when the pain of drinking is worse than not drinking. Bottoming out indicates the point where alcoholics are motivated to get better or to give up. A bottom is the time when a person is in crisis: to be or not to be, to become sober or to continue drinking, live a marginal existence, be institutionalized, or die.

Alcoholics who do change and recover often experience a "low bottom." They come to a point where life is falling apart, where there are numerous negative consequences to self and others, where they are powerless and have difficulty managing. A "low bottom" usually means that there is disruptive and dysfunctional behavior along with significant losses such as the loss of a spouse, children, family, religion, friends, and job and/or physical, emotional, cognitive, and spiritual deterioration. Such a low bottom can motivate alcoholics to stop drinking and get sober, for the alternative is usually a marginal existence, institutionalization, or early death.

A problem is that normal alcoholics often manage to function without experiencing such a bottom. In contrast to a low bottom syndrome, normal alcoholics are successful at work, their marriages and children seem to function well, they are active in the community and church, and are often admired. Consequently, instead of "hitting a low bottom," they maintain a relative "high" level of functionality and comfort. Unlike the lives of low bottom, abnormal alcoholics, their life is unlikely to pressure them to change. Few people change significantly without being motivated by pain. Normal alcoholics manage to live with and numb their pain as well as have enough success and pleasure to compensate for the pain. In short, there is not enough reason or pain to change.

Not hitting a bottom has its assets and deficits. On the positive side of the ledger, normal alcoholics do not usually experience as much pain and/or destruction to self and others. On the negative side, it is much easier for them to deceive themselves as well as be enabled by others. So, since most alcoholics manage to live with their alcoholism and since most people deny and enable their disorder, alcoholics seldom enter a recovery program.

If hitting bottom is the usual way to come to admit being alcoholic, if such acceptance is necessary in order to recover, and if normal alcoholics and others can easily deny and rationalize their alcoholic behavior, then how can normal alcoholics recover? Rather than waiting for a low bottom, the challenge is to be willing and able to recognize the negative consequences of normal alcoholism in order to experience a "high bottom" that leads to recovery. Listen to Mike who had such an experience.

"I'm still not sure why I quit drinking and started sobriety. Unlike many of my A.A. friends, I didn't get in trouble or undergo permanent losses, but somehow I felt I was losing my dignity. I didn't feel good about myself living two lives — one that was responsible and the other drinking. I realized I spent too much time drinking, felt too tired, withdrew too much, and simply didn't feel healthy. I began to wonder if life could be better, and I felt an internal pressure to try out life without drinking. My feeling proved to be right; I'm better off without drinking."

Few alcoholics come to accept their alcoholism and begin recovery as "easily" as Mike. Many have to travel a long road of non-acceptance — such as denial, rationalization, and collusion as well as cognitive/behavioral/affective deterioration, isolation, and spiritual desolation — before they are willing and able to recover. Many more maintain their alcoholism, slowly burn out, or quit drinking but remain (dry) drunk.

A difficulty is that we seldom try to help normal alcoholics until they are dysfunctional or cause problems to self and others. When people can manage, we seldom bother with or become concerned about them. To help people who are functional, we must recognize the existence of normal alcoholism (in self and/ or others), and then make the necessary changes to become sober. Indeed, acceptance and recovery are easier said than done.

Summary Remarks

Most alcoholics are more normal than abnormal; they maintain relative control and manage relatively well. They do not stand out as abnormal or dysfunctional persons; they do well at work and recreation. Although they usually have difficulty with intimacy, most "normal" people have such problems. These alcoholics are seen and judged to be normal, functional, in control, frequently successful, and sometimes admired. They are rarely called sick, abnormal, or alcoholic.

But, they are alcoholic because alcohol plays a central role in their life. Normal alcoholics obsess about drinking, and they feel compelled to drink particularly when under stress and/or when it is "time to drink." Drinking is simply on their minds and in their guts too much and too often. Although the negative effects of their drinking may be subtle, they still outweigh the positive effects. The negative consequences are mostly centered around the spiritual and/or intimate dimensions of life. Although they may manage to avoid falling into the low bottom of dysfunctionality, their so-called high bottom is deceptive and precarious.

Although normal alcoholics may not be addicted in the sense of undergoing serious metabolic, cellular changes and physical withdrawal symptoms, they are nevertheless alcoholic. Normal alcoholics do not easily fit the classic description or syndrome of the alcoholic, namely, the person who has a progressive, chronic, primary, and fatal disease, or the person who is out of control. Although they may progress in drinking, the progression usually occurs over decades, or it may not progress. Nevertheless, alcohol impedes their functioning; they obsess about and feel compelled to drink; they fail to learn from their abusive habits; and their presence to self, others, and God is impeded. But as long as they manage to be normal, recovery is unlikely.

4 Normal Alcoholics

In light of the preceding stories and definitions of alcoholism, we will now explore different styles of being normal and alcoholic. These thematic variations can also contribute to our understanding and treatment of alcoholism.

Polished Alcoholics

"Polished" alcoholics are arguably the most normal, functional, successful, and admired as well as deceptive and seductive alcoholics. These alcoholics are polished: smooth, refined, and cultured, often manifesting a luster and gloss that others admire. They are invariably articulate, well groomed, seemingly confident, and mentally sharp. In their public roles they know their lines well, and they usually manage to give highly rated performances.

Such alcoholic performers rarely fit a common conception of alcoholics — sloppy, gross, shabby, dull, or out of control. Instead, they manage to achieve their professional goals and often are good to others. For example, consider politicians who drink alcoholically and yet manage to help their constituents. Some psychotherapists help their patients in spite of their own alcoholism. Alcoholic priests and ministers are usually good persons who effectively minister, teach, lead, and celebrate. Indeed, professional people helpers can be competent and compassionate, yet drink alcoholically.

Polished alcoholics cultivate the art of drinking with grace and precision to achieve relaxation for extended and manageable times. They are skilled at stopping just short of an unmanageable "buzz" that impedes their refined demeanor. When they go beyond their boundaries, they manage to vanish from the scene — buying time to sober up. Seldom is their polished performance publicly tarnished.

Listen to Rex. "After twenty-six months of sobriety and attending A.A. meetings two or three times a week, I still can't fully admit or surrender to the fact of being an alcoholic. However, I can admit that my drinking caused more negative than positive effects and that I am better off not drinking. If that makes me an alcoholic, then I guess I am.

"Sure, my life was far from being perfectly clean. My main fault was being too much in my own world, and I know this had an effect on my wife and kids. My absence made a difference. Yet, I could get on stage and captivate audiences for hours at a time. How could such a person be an alcoholic? How could a famous person who inspires people be an alcoholic?

"Relatively easy. I would control my drinking so that I could lecture and write well. For instance, while writing, I would drink to relax for a considerable time, and when I got too mellow, I would simply stop writing and doze off. When I gave a talk, I would never drink until after my presentation. And if there was a cocktail hour before my talk, I would abstain.

"None of my colleagues, friends, or anyone would label me an alcoholic, more likely they would say that I liked to drink and have a good time. I was the life of the party; I would engage in serious and light dialogue as well as join in the fun without being disruptive. Actually, my gifts helped me to hide my disorder. In fact, the wives of my alcoholic friends knew that their husbands wouldn't get in any trouble as long as they were with me. Almost everyone admired and held me up as a role model.

"So, why am I an alcoholic? Well, although I was trying to be sincere, I was not entirely honest. Not that I purposely lied, but I fooled people and especially myself. And as I said before, I am certain that I am better off not drinking. I relate better, I enjoy life much more, I share my feelings better, and I am a clearer thinker. More importantly, I don't feel so sneaky and shameful as I once did; I feel more integrity. Furthermore, other people who are close to me, like my wife and children, say that I am a better person since I've stopped drinking. I am more consistent, present, and caring. Although at times I don't feel much of a difference between now and then, I have to respect and trust their opinion. I don't want to deceive myself again.

"In other simple but important ways I know that I'm better off. For example, when I used to go to the theater, I would go with a couple of drinks in me, have a couple drinks during the play, and a couple after. While watching the first act I would be pleasantly aware, in the second act it was as if I were in a fog, and in the third act I fought or fell asleep. And I usually had difficulty recalling the total play. Now, I am more alert, and I enjoy and recall the experience better. Indeed, life is still difficult at times, but overall I am better."

Closet Alcoholics

Closet alcoholics are the secret and silent drinkers. They are probably the last people on earth that you would consider to be an alcoholic, for their drinking is done in private. They enter their closet, close the door, lock it from the inside, and drink. Drinking within the safe confines of isolation protects them from being seen. And they rarely come out of their drinking closet unless they are quite functional. Abstaining from being involved and keeping to themselves, their alcoholic self is hidden from almost everyone. Such is their control.

Their drinking tends to be planned, measured, timed, and

structured. For instance, they schedule times to drink. Some might drink only at night or only after work and others only on weekends, perhaps beginning late Friday afternoon and ending early Sunday night. They avoid public drinking. For example, at a wedding, they drink little or not at all, but when they return home, they drink privately. Thus, they maintain and project the illusion of being sober.

Think of the monk who never drank except secretly in his room. He was articulate at meals, active in ministry, and dependable and trustworthy; consequently, no one would identify him as being an alcoholic. Although he would usually abstain from drinking at the community's cocktail hour, after dinner he would retire to his room, begin to drink, and fall asleep with a pleasant high.

In some respects, many alcoholics are closet or hidden alcoholics. They control, plan, and manage to hide their drinking. Again, why is such drinking alcoholic? Why is the successful monk who drinks before retiring an alcoholic? Indeed, he functions as well or better than most people. The diagnostic issue, however, is not just a matter of what he does or when and how much he drinks. The issue is also that alcohol leads, however covertly, to negative consequences in his thinking, feeling, and behavior. Indeed, his spiritual life is also negatively influenced.

Being sober, the monk would be better off physically such as not being so tired and vulnerable to illness. He would be an even more efficient worker, producing more and being just as or more creative. More importantly, he would be a better community member and be more spiritually present.

Most alcoholics of whatever kind have difficulty with intimacy, for their being in love with alcohol impedes their relationships with people. Alcohol numbs feelings, fogs thinking, and constricts judgment. Although this monk usually functions well with people and practices a spiritual life, his interpersonal and spiritual life would improve with sobriety. Alcohol simply disrupts his presence to others, including God.

Listen to this housewife. "No one would say that I was an alcoholic, with the exception of my husband. I was an educated person with a Psy.D. Although I had been in private practice, I chose to leave private practice to be full time with my children. During that time, I began to drink in a consistent and predictable pattern. For instance, I waited until my children arrived home from school, got settled, and went out to play; then I would start to drink. Every day at 4:00 p.m., I would start drinking so that when my husband came home at 6:00 p.m., I was pleasantly high. Before that, I would do house and volunteer work, be socially involved, and read. After eating dinner, I rarely drank, except if my husband and I went out. Normally, I would clean up after dinner, read, watch some television, and retire.

"I have been sober for five and a half years; I'm also back in private practice. When I look back at my drinking problem, I can understand some of the reasons for my drinking, such as neutralizing my ambivalent feelings toward my husband. Since then, I have entered psychotherapy and have worked through many of my feelings. Somewhat simplistically stated, I used to drink to cope with my fears and low self-esteem as well as hostility toward my husband and men in general.

"I functioned fairly well, but at some expense to my children. Although they didn't have the name alcoholic, they knew that something was peculiar, and it had something to do with drinking between 4:00 and 6:00 o'clock. I might add that my kids have apparently worked out well. They haven't gotten in any trouble, they don't drink as far as I know, and they have done quite well in school and other activities. I am proud of them, and I thank God that they didn't follow my way. At least not yet.

"I vaguely knew that I drank too much. Although I told myself I could quit at any time, I always found myself drinking between 4:00 and 6:00 p.m. Indeed, I could abstain for days, or even weeks at a time, but I knew that I would come back to drinking again. And I always did. Thus, I sort of played games with myself, knowing that I had problems. But I never identified myself as being alcoholic. Good grief — I was a highly educated, diagnostically hip, socially adept, model mother, wife, and woman!

"The experience that probably pushed me over the edge happened when we drove 400 miles to visit the college my oldest child was planning to attend. Before we began the trip, I did something different that day: I had a Bloody Mary for breakfast, a couple more for lunch, and a Vodka when we arrived at the motel. Unusual, but not spectacular. When we visited the school, I apparently was my sophisticated self, and when we returned to the motel, I must have continued to drink. The unusual thing was that when my husband asked about the trip the next day, I could recall relatively little. This floored me. Since then, I haven't touched a drop.

"Soon after, I began to read about alcoholism, and I attended some A.A. meetings. It took me about two years before I realized that I stood on common ground with the other alcoholics. What especially helped me to feel at home was what A.A. calls service work. Simple acts like setting up tables and chairs, making coffee, and emptying ash trays broke down my isolationism as well as my professional elitism.

"I still don't find many stories like my own — of the closet alcoholic homemaker. Most of the stories have low, dramatic, and often public bottoms. They are not as smooth and silent as mine. I wonder how many women there are like me with no place to go except in a closet.

"Again, I got in no difficulty with the law and my children are in good shape, but my marriage did end. I think my marriage ended because of my alcoholism but also because of other factors that the alcoholism hid. Sadly enough, I think Ted and I were simply not suited to be married to each other. Whether that is true or not, I know that life has improved now that I am sober."

Periodic Alcoholics

Periodic alcoholics can go days, months, and years without drinking. Some, for example, abstain at certain times of the year; others drink for years, then abstain for years, and again resume their alcoholic drinking.

During these periods of abstinence, they are not necessarily sober. They still behave alcoholically. It is as if they are on hold, waiting to resume drinking. In fact, people who live with dry alcoholics sometimes wish they would start drinking again because they prefer their mellow and passive wet self rather than their irritable and disruptive dry self. As one co-alcoholic said, "At least when my husband is drinking, he's mellow and falls asleep and doesn't cause any big time trouble. When he's not drinking, he starts arguments, criticizes, and is just difficult to live with. Indeed, I don't want him to drink, but I'd also like him to be more pleasant when he's sober."

Being normal, periodic alcoholics can put on a good show; nevertheless, they are out to lunch much of the time — being less present than they could be. In particular, their life of intimacy suffers.

Listen to Dan, a periodic alcoholic who is not in recovery. "Me, an alcoholic? Come on now. I haven't had a drink for Lent in the past 23 years. Isn't that proof positive that I'm not an alcoholic? And did you see me drunk at the last wedding? No way; I was as sober as you. My view of an alcoholic is someone who loses control. You know, as they say in A.A.: One drink is too many and a thousand is not enough. That certainly doesn't apply to me. Furthermore, I can't recall the last time I got drunk or sick from booze.

"And I've quit many times for long periods of time. One time I quit for two-and-a-half years, and when I started to drink again, I drank normally. Usually I drink four or five bottles of beer after work and probably a case or so on the weekend. Compared to my buddies, I'm a piker. Number one: I just drink beer. Number two: I don't drink nearly as much as many of my friends. And three: I do stop to prove to myself that I have control.

"Listen, I went to a couple of A.A. meetings because I thought I might have a drinking problem. But after hearing their stories, I was sure that I wasn't an alcoholic. They talked about losing their families, their jobs, being violently aggressive, sneaking drinks, getting into financial problems, and in general doing crazy things. They repeatedly talked about their loss of control. I simply don't fit their description of being an alcoholic. I never missed a day of work, never got into any trouble with the law, my marriage is okay, my family is doing well, I'm in good financial condition, and I continue to do okay. Sure, I do like to drink, but I deserve some rewards for working so hard. A few bottles of beer helps to take the edge off things."

Now listen to Dan's wife, Lois. "I don't know if Dan is an alcoholic or not, but I know that when he's drinking, he's difficult to live with. Although he meets most of his responsibilities, he is usually off in his own world. Although he says he never really gets drunk or sick, he's not up to par; it's as if he is not quite present.

"I appreciate that Dan never goes out to bars. And I can depend on him to be faithful and financially responsible. But I can't depend on him being intimate with me. Have you ever tried to make love or just be intimate with someone who has beer on his breath or is fighting sleep? Yuck! And although our children don't hate their father, neither do they really know him. He's sort of a nice guy who lives in the shadows. Everyone thinks Dan is a nice guy, and in many ways he is. But it's simply difficult living with a phantom.

"Furthermore, I'm really not sure if I like Dan when he's not drinking. When he stops, he is just as bad or worse. At least when he's drinking, he's less troublesome. When he's not drinking, he is tense and irritable, and actually more difficult to live with. At least when he's passed out in his chair, I don't have to worry about or deal with him."

Borderline Alcoholics

A popular model of alcoholism differentiates four types of drinkers: experimenters, social drinkers, abusers, and alcoholics or addicts. This system's key diagnostic factor is "control." For instance, most people have "tried" alcohol and maintained control without an urge or desire to drink again. Such experimenters simply seldom drink again or give much thought to it. Social drinkers can take it or leave it without difficulty. They, too, exercise control. And there are persons who abuse alcohol and experience negative consequences, but they exercise some control and are not physically dependent on alcohol. In contrast, alcoholics are addictively dependent on alcohol, lose control, and consequently fail to manage adequately. In our context, although "abusers" do not lose control, they are nevertheless alcoholics and often the borderline type.

While abusing alcohol, borderline alcoholics manage their drinking so they can behave normally. Despite being subtly obsessed with alcohol and feeling compelled to drink, they manage to cope rather well. And when they get out of bounds, they quickly return to and remain within normal boundaries. Although they seldom cause public disruption, such an "in and out" movement is tiresome to self and to others.

Borderline alcoholics walk a chalk line. They test limits, and when they go beyond the boundaries of normality, they fall back into line. They usually manage to stay out of serious trouble, and when they do cause trouble, they manage to apologize, cover-up, and cope normally.

As with many alcoholics, their personal life is often different from their public life. Spouse and children as well as other people who are close to them see and hear a different story. Although borderline alcoholics are often constant drinkers who manage to work productively and be socially and financially responsible, their private lives are restricted. Their consistent drinking exacts a cost to themselves and others, particularly in the more personal and interpersonal realms.

As time goes on, intimacy dissipates and their physical, mental, and spiritual condition suffers. Moving deeper into alcoholism, hangovers become more frequent and intense, memory is impaired, feelings are blunted, energy level is lowered. Borderline alcoholics often cross the border between normal and abnormal drinking.

Consider Pam, a single, career woman who is also a borderline alcoholic. "Yes, I admit that I drink too much. I know I have martini lunches and I spend too many evenings at a bar. So I like to relax with a couple of drinks before I have dinner. Why not? I work very hard. Furthermore, it is not easy to be a single woman in the corporate sexist world, and yes: I am lonely at times. I have only had a couple of affairs, and I know that they're not the way to meet my needs. So, when I get too lonely or empty, I drink. It's better than getting involved in a dead-end relationship, and it beats feeling pain.

"I admit I have a problem, but I'm not an alcoholic. Yes, my boss did mention to me that I might be drinking too much, but he assured me that my work is more than adequate. He was just concerned about my drinking. And I, too, am concerned, but I work hard and I don't have much fun in life. Drinking helps me to relax and lessen tension. Why shouldn't I have some drinks to feel high and not so damn low? What's the big deal? What harm is there?"

Pam, like most normal alcoholics, drinks more than she realizes as well as denies and minimizes the harm she inflicts on herself and others. Pam has difficulty enjoying life and having fun without alcohol. Rather than moving over the border to unmanageable alcoholism, her challenge is to move the other way toward sobriety.

Compliant Alcoholics

Compliant alcoholics are perhaps the easiest to enable and most difficult to help because they are such "nice" and disarming people. These pleasing people keep the rules, defer to others, and stay out of conflict. They move pleasantly toward or away from others, always avoiding difficulties. Consider some of the variations of these compliant alcoholics.

Many compliant alcoholics are "mellow." They make efforts to be congenial, gentle, understanding, and sympathetic, and are seldom harsh or disruptive. Being soft and friendly, they are easy to approach, and they listen to others. And since they seldom are argumentative or oppositional, they are easy to be with. Understandably, mellow alcoholics are usually liked and are seldom seen as alcoholics.

On the other hand, if you live with a mellow alcoholic, you probably have a different experience. Although they do not cause much trouble, neither are they very helpful, honest, confrontational, exciting, or intimate. Being passive and pleasant and abhorring conflict, they seldom take initiative, give feedback, or work through conflict. People who live with mellow alcoholics often become bored or fed up with their passive and obsequious style.

Another variation of the compliant alcoholic is the "withdrawn and avoidant" alcoholic. Withdrawn alcoholics are simply in their own worlds; they drink and keep to themselves. Since they stay out of any kind of conflictual, confrontational, or oppositional interaction, they remain harmless and "nice." Rather than being aggressive or even assertive, they avoid any kind of conflict and seek "peace" at any price. Although they are not outgoing or particularly pleasing people, neither are they displeasing.

Listen to Harry. "When I was drinking, I never got into any arguments or caused any trouble. I simply would come home and drink until I fell asleep. On weekends, I would start drinking Friday night and stop Sunday night. I went to our basement and watched sports all weekend, and I managed to fit household chores and duties around my drinking and watching television. I would shop on Saturday during a break between games, and I took the family to church Sunday morning. From the outside, I was seen as a model husband and father. Indeed, I was not that bad, but neither was I that good."

Being so passive and compliant, these alcoholics are difficult to criticize. Although their compliant and avoidant demeanor disarms people, there are negative consequences. Simply not being present causes problems. For example, when Harry is in the basement watching sports alcoholically, he is not with his wife and children. His absence becomes an irritating and dysfunctional presence. Interpersonal relationships, which are essential to healthy living, are inconsistent and unreliable.

More present and "pleasing" alcoholics are willing to do anything for others as long as others are nice to them. Their main goal is to please people so that people like them. Thus, they are the "easy touch" in the family, willing to give and do anything so they can avoid being disliked, to erase conflict, and to engender being liked. Being always ready to do anything for anyone, they run after others like hungry puppies begging for a bone or a pat on the head. Since the gratification of their needs depends on others, they actually empower others and feel less in control. And when their needs are not met, they are likely to become angry, passive aggressive, or resentful. Such insecurity and dependent behavior lend themselves to drinking alcoholically.

Most compliant alcoholics are prone to guilt and low self-esteem. When people are displeased with them, they automatically wonder what they did wrong and search for ways to make things right, and being so dependent, they place their worth in other people's hands. Their shame-based position compels them to pressure others to like them, or they simply avoid being seen. In both cases, they do not feel worthy of what they want and need: to be loved and to feel worthwhile. When they hurt too much, they drink a little extra to numb their pain of guilt, low self-esteem, and shame.

Many compliant alcoholics are ready and willing to take the blame for anything. If you criticize them, they plead guilty, yet their self-blame and willingness to plead guilty disarms others. Such contrition, however, can be manipulative and passively aggressive — an attempt to provoke guilt and sorrow as well as getting what they want. And if their unconscious ploys fail to work, they can feel nourished, loved, and at "peace" via drinking.

Another variation of this theme is a "stoic" alcoholic — one who holds in feelings, plays the suffering martyr role, and gets people to feel sorry for him. Since stoic alcoholics often take on considerable responsibility, they and their friends rationalize that drinking is an understandable way to ease the pain that comes with life's burdens.

Patrick, a stoic alcoholic, was married to a woman who was chronically depressed with periodic manic episodes. His bi-polar wife would occasionally act out and go on buying sprees that put Patrick in debt, and at other times she was depressed, withdrawn, morbid, hysterical, and paranoid. Everybody knew that Patrick's wife was mentally ill and extremely difficult to live with; however, Patrick never complained. He would cope with and cater to his wife, and would medicate and drink himself to sleep after his wife went to bed.

In public, he would seldom overdrink, but when he did, people certainly understood. They admired Patrick for his care of and responsibility toward his wife, and they excused his tendency to drink "a bit" too much. More importantly, Patrick rationalized his own drinking by thinking that anyone would drink with a wife like his, and furthermore, God would understand and even want him to drink. God, Patrick rationalized, is compassionate. Indeed, Patrick was very active in church and was admired by church people and his minister. Listen to Patrick who has since entered recovery.

"Although I was sincere in the way I treated my wife, I nevertheless deceived myself and others; namely, I would justify my drinking because of the stress in my life. Now that I'm not drinking and have been in recovery for four years, I can deal with my wife's illness much better than when I was drinking. Furthermore, my stoicism and drinking numbed my feelings so that I was out of touch with myself. Although my religious activity was sincere, it was not as good as it is now. Not only is my mind in my religion but now my heart is there too.

"I've also learned to let go of the resentment I had toward my wife. I realize that my alcoholic stoicism served to cover and numb my deep anger toward her. When my anger tried to surface, I drank more. I guess I had to be a good guy — one who is always caring and never angry, and drinking helped me play that role. Now I am really learning to be a good guy, not just a caricature of one.

"What really irritated me is when she denied her illness and blamed her misery on others, including me. As long as I needed her to stop blaming and be responsible, I was in deep trouble. I've learned to accept her nonacceptance. More importantly, I've come to accept my own illness, and with the help of God, I can progress."

Some compliant alcoholics combine a gift for being "humorous" with drinking. Since they are funny and often the life of the party, nearly everyone wants to be around them. However, although their public persona is entertaining, their private, darker side is not always humorous.

Listen to the wife of a humorous alcoholic. "It really galled me to see my husband being the life of the party and really a funny guy. It galled me because as soon as we would leave to go home, he would change personalities. He was like Dr. Jekyll and Mr. Hyde. From being a really funny guy, he became quiet and withdrawn, and sometimes aggressive and abusive. He simply did not know how to function when he was not on stage. It seemed as if he used his humor to hide his true self. It was as if he were like a clown, and when he took off his suit and makeup, he was a scared and angry man.

"After many years of being eaten alive with anger, I joined Al-Anon and learned to deal with my husband and even to enjoy his humor when he was in public. Acceptance and loving detachment were critical to my recovery. When I no longer needed my husband to change, I stopped trying to control him and started to manage more effectively. Detaching from and refusing to enable his alcoholic behavior helped me to hurt much less and to be freer. Letting Jack take responsibility for himself actually helped him. And I learned to be responsible and to care for myself.

"And you know what? He began to express some humor with me, and I learned to enjoy him in his good times and accept him and manage when he was silent or aggressive. Although I never condoned his drinking or negative behavior, I learned to enjoy him. I learned to love him as an alcoholic, although I detested his alcoholism. Hopefully someday he will become a sober funny man."

Oppositional Alcoholics

In contrast to compliant alcoholics who are ready to follow rules and avoid conflict, oppositional alcoholics are people who resist, contradict, and become aggressive. Rather than being compliant with or avoiding others, they actively oppose, control, or dominate others.

The most recognizable oppositional alcoholics are explicitly aggressive and often hostile. Needing others to agree with them, they are argumentative and often provoke verbal fights. Their point of view is the only one, and if you disagree, you are simply wrong. They will argue, shout, and insult. And if you are not intimidated, they sometimes cry, and if tears do not work, they withdraw in contempt. They do anything to win. Arbitrary rightness characterizes their style. Their self-esteem or lack of it seems to depend on winning arguments, telling people what to do, or overall: being in control. Their defense is to have a very aggressive offense.

Listen to Debra. "God I don't know how people put up with me. I was so adept at winning arguments, especially with men who seemed chauvinistic or arrogant. I got great delight in showing them up and putting them down. I knew how to pull their chain, particularly the men who were uncertain of their masculinity and felt compelled to engage me in battle. And this is what I loved — to beat men at their own game. Interestingly, although I was known as a real bitch, men seemed to be challenged by and attracted to me.

"The thing that I regret most is arguing with and putting down my husband. For example, when we were in a restaurant, I would often become argumentative, make a scene with my abusive language, and insult him. In social settings, I would bring up personal issues in front of others to embarrass him. I couldn't stand my husband's success or even people liking him. This threatened me, and I felt compelled to criticize him. It is as if I had to put him down so I could feel up.

"Furthermore, when there was trouble in the family or with the children, I would blame him. I would criticize him for being too passive, unfeeling, not taking enough responsibility, and for undermining my authority. Keep in mind that any view that differed from mine was seen as usurping my authority. He could never be right unless he agreed with me. And when he did agree, I'd call him a wimp for not having a view of his own. Of course, I rarely if ever criticized myself, and I would never say that I was wrong. And on the rare occasion when I did admit to wrong doing, I made excuses and eventually blamed others for my less than perfect behavior.

"I would always blame others. Others were responsible for my unhappiness, for my ill health, for my not working, for being fired, etc., etc. Negative comments far outweighed the positive, and I would justify my negativity by rationalizing that I was simply being honest. I would drive my husband nuts by telling him how he really felt even though he said he didn't feel the way I said. Then I would accuse him of denial, repression, and an inability to communicate.

"Since being sober for the past three and a half years and getting some useful psychotherapy, I came to discover that I've always been very angry at men, and often for good reasons. To make a very long and painful story short, my two brothers sexually abused me, my father abused me with his alcoholism, and my mother withdrew in fear. Consequently, I built an enormous slush fund of resentment toward men and women. And drinking enabled me to express my anger and repress my shame. In fact, I often had little or no recognition of my abusive behavior. Indeed, to some extent I did the very thing that hurt me. Although I still have a way to go, I'm on my way and I'm healing."

Pete has a different story. "When I was drinking, I rarely lost control at work. Since I simply couldn't afford to be argumentative or insulting with my business colleagues, I controlled myself. Home was another matter.

"With my wife and children I would shout, scream, insult, abuse, and just be an obnoxious schmuck. Although I never, thank God, physically abused my wife and children, I came close to it. But I did verbally abuse them. I would call my children names like dumb, inferior, lazy, ask them what's wrong with them, and overall put them down. I would take great delight in making fun of my wife such as telling her she was overweight, not competent enough to hold a job, and that she had an easy life. Really, I was obnoxious. I don't know how my family stood me. No, I know how they stood me: They tolerated me at a great price."

Other oppositional alcoholics are not as explicitly abusive, but are aggressive in a passive and indirect way. They are "passive aggressive," like being indifferent and behaving irritably.

Since their anger is seldom expressed explicitly, passive

aggressive people rarely become explosive like argumentative and aggressive alcoholics. In fact, publicly they are often nice people, but privately they express their enormous anger passively and indirectly. And when their behavior is pointed out to them, they deny or minimize it. Thus, it is difficult to deal and live with such people.

Others become skilled at undermining another's authority. For example, although they may never explicitly criticize their spouse's viewpoint and behavior, neither do they give it support. They are adept at becoming the good person and making the other (spouse) the bad person. For instance, a man may seldom say that his wife is wrong, but he is more likely to state that people have to "understand" and "tolerate" her, or even pray for her. The point is that he does not give support but subtly undermines her.

Sheldon was a classic passive-aggressive and pleasing alcoholic. "It is amazing how I manipulated people with my pleasing and passive behavior. When my wife would complain about me forgetting to do something or for not listening, I immediately pleaded guilty and promised that I would never do it again. I would disarm her with my contrition, try to make her feel guilty for her hostility, and would change my ways but not for long. Playing the role of the long-suffering martyr was manipulative and hostile.

"When my children complained about me not having enough time for them, I said that I was sorry but I couldn't help it because I was working so hard for them and because I had to rest so that I'd have energy to make money for them. And I always assured them that I would try harder and to do my best. Or I promised them that I would take them somewhere special on the weekend — and sometimes I did and sometimes I didn't. But I wasn't consistent, nor did I take their complaints seriously for very long. Everyone thought I was a nice guy, and I really did try. I loved my kids, but I loved booze a little bit more. You know, I always managed to make time for alcohol.

"When people began to complain too much about me, I

would go to my mother. She was always sympathetic about how hard people were on me. How could people criticize me? I was faithful, held down a job, did chores, was nice, and was ready to plead guilty. And I was always ready to improve, but seldom did my improvements last. I would give the appearance of sorrow and sobriety but it was only an act, not intentional but nevertheless real. Indeed, I was sincere in my efforts to improve, but drinking was a little more important."

Consider the alcoholic woman who behaves passive-aggressively by playing the suffering martyr. She seldom gives her husband support or affirmation, but rather "mildly" complains about him and her children to almost everyone. She "negativises" them by maximizing their negativity along with minimizing their positivity. And when she drinks more than usual, she is likely to, as it were, cry in her beer and talk for hours about how bad her life is. "Poor me" is the negative lament: "Why is life so unfair? Why can't my family do the right things? I try so hard to help them. Maybe some day, they'll see the light. I'll continue to pray for them."

Some oppositional alcoholics tend to be hysterical: They gush with emotion, are overly affective, and are great at putting on a show of being hurt, helpless, and maligned. These alcoholics will often evoke sympathy by crying about their oppressive and unfair situation. Other alcoholics may just lose control — screaming, shouting, and eventually crying, and then rationalize their extreme behavior by stating that they are simply expressing their feelings. Or they might justify themselves by saying that they need to ventilate their feelings or that they are being honest as if expression of "honesty" justifies hurting others. Actually their emotive expression is too often an exercise in narcissism at the expense of the other persons's rights and feelings.

Rachel was a functional alcoholic who was oppositional and hysterical. Especially when drinking, she would express intense anger and hurt feelings, followed by tears, and finally hostile withdrawal. She bottled up her feelings and let them out when she was overdrinking. Sometimes when she was relatively sober, she could express some of her anger, but could never get at the underlying pain and shame that her anger covered. Only after working an A.A. program did she enter therapy to uncover the source of her rage and shame: incest.

Holy Alcoholics

Although being a holy alcoholic may sound like a contradiction, it is not rare. Some people are genuinely holy: They do good, abstain from evil, pray to God or a Higher Power, try to be virtuous, and overall try to live a spiritual life. To be sure, they are far from being perfect, and one of their biggest imperfections is alcoholism and its underlying self-will and self-reliance.

Actually, it is possible to be a sick saint — and, there have been more than a few. (Holiness is not the same as healthiness, although true healthiness includes holiness.) For instance, people can be alcoholic (or obsessive-compulsive, dependent, depressed, phobic, etc.) and be holy. In what ways and how much alcoholism and/or psychopathology impacts on holy living is another topic worthy of a book. In general, however, it can be said that problems can challenge and impede one's spiritual life and that spirituality can help one to cope and heal.

As we said in Chapter One, religious ministers can be good and effective persons who preach the Word of God, care for God's people, and help them to celebrate God's presence, while drinking alcoholically. And there are vowed religious women and men who are holy alcoholics. Unfortunately such persons usually get help only when they have crossed the border from normal functioning to more disruptive behavior. In fact, there are special residential treatment centers for such clerical and religious alcoholics.

Perhaps it is difficult to imagine a nun being an alcoholic. Although it is not common, neither is it extremely rare. Listen to Sister Martha. "I still get a little embarrassed when I think of my drinking days. In short, I managed to be a very good teacher and later one of the best principals while being an active alcoholic. How? In some respects it was easy, and in other ways it was difficult.

"Alcohol was not always easy to get. That's one of the drawbacks of a nun's life, at least for an alcoholic. But when you're an alcoholic, you learn to be ingenious and to manage. I would meekly ask people for a bottle of spirits for Christmas, Easter, birthday. Or if people simply wanted to show their gratitude, I would suggest alcohol, implying that it was for medical purposes and/or to share with the community. And, I would be careful about keeping everyone in a state of ignorance; that is, no one knew what the others were buying. Furthermore, no one except God would ever consider me to be an alcoholic.

"Anyhow, along with these gifts my dear, alcoholic father and enabling mother would always buy some spirits for their spiritual daughter. Furthermore, I returned to my community only a small portion of the considerable gift monies I received so that I had a good stock of money and booze.

"Being a good disciplined nun, I had certain iron clad rules: only one drink in public, never drink when there was school the next day, and do most of my drinking in private. After dinner, I would socialize with my community and after evening prayer I would retire to my room and drink. Although I practiced the religious life and for the most part was a good sister, alcohol — not God — was my primary comforter and source of happiness. I did not live according to Divine Providence, but alcohol became my God. I would never admit to this, but my life told a different story. Now God is Comforter and Consoler."

Indeed, you need not be a religious or minister to be a "holy alcoholic." Many lay people are genuinely holy people as well as alcoholic. They believe in God and/or a Reality greater than themselves, try to do good and help others, and live a spiritual and virtuous life. Then why quit drinking? Because, recovering holy alcoholics will attest that the quality and effectiveness of their life and ministry improved when they became sober.

Their life of love is more real — less theoretical, controlling, and isolated and more experiential, open, and interpersonal. Often the presence of God becomes more practical and helpful in everyday living. No longer having to live two lives, they feel freer and more honest and truthful. Depending on a Reality greater than their individual selves liberates, strengthens, and nourishes them to be better holy people.

In this chapter, variations of the theme of normal alcoholism have been described and analyzed. We have seen that normal alcoholism can be manifested in various ways, usually as a function of the individual's personality structure.

A common theme is that most alcoholics deceive themselves with the delusion of perfect contentment. Some try to reach perfection and consequent illusionary control by pleasing, complying, being mellow, or simply avoiding conflict. Others try to gain perfection by aggressively forcing people to act according to their will. They gain security by trying to control the situation, while others gain security by pleasing and complying. Still other alcoholics try to be perfectly safe and secure by avoiding much of life and simply staying in their own world. On the basis of our stories and analyses, let us consider the "positive" and negative consequences of normal alcoholism.

5 Positive and Negative Consequences

Alcoholism, whatever type, makes sense and nonsense. Few people drink to feel worse; indeed, they drink to "feel better." In particular, alcoholics/addicts tend to totalize the "sense" of drinking while denying or minimizing the "nonsense." To increase the likelihood of recovery in self and/or others, it is important to accept and understand both the sense and nonsense — the positive and negative consequences of alcoholic drinking.

Some people might question the prudence of discussing the sense of drinking alcoholically. Some believe that such talk could enable alcoholics to rationalize and justify their drinking, while others contend that alcoholism makes no sense or that it is a completely negative experience. I think that recognition of the sense in the nonsense of alcoholic drinking can facilitate recovery. Recovery often necessitates acceptance of and mourning the loss of alcoholic meaning as well as compensation for these losses.

Positive Consequences

Alcoholics drink because it makes sense. In many ways alcoholics can "feel" better when drinking, but only for a temporary period of time. Sooner or later, these apparent assets lead to deficits. If there were no negative consequences, drinking alcoholically might be justified.

Drinking alcoholically can make considerable sense. For instance, it offers a sense of fulfillment — a feeling that everything is together and all right. Particularly when it causes many people to feel as if they have no problems, or they experience a sense of serenity, albeit a pseudo sense that neither lasts nor is freely engendered from within themselves. Nevertheless, alcohol gives a counterfeit feeling of calm, peace, and comfort. When drinking, everything is on euphoric hold.

As we have seen and will continue to see, alcoholics (and all addicts) usually seek "heavenly states" — perpetual contentment, fulfillment, bliss, and balance as well as perfect courage, intimacy, harmony, and serenity. Experiencing an illusory touch of heaven is one of the main reasons alcoholics continue to drink despite the negative consequences. So, to become sober, one must face and replace the alcoholically induced illusions with healthier and more realistic experiences.

Alcohol can be especially alluring to people with chronic problems. If a person suffers from problems like obsessive-compulsive behavior and/or anxiety disorders, alcohol can give relief. Alcohol can enable repressed people to express themselves, avoidant persons to assert themselves, and pleasers to tolerate conflict. And, the painful diminishment of shame can be numbed and hidden with alcohol. However, such attempts at freeing oneself from psychological prisons are contingent on returning to prison. Although alcohol can anesthetize uncomfortable symptoms, give repose from ineffective behavior, and offer self-nourishment, the negative consequences are sooner or later greater than the positive ones. To cope and nourish with alcohol usually does more harm than good.

Nevertheless, alcohol can give an illusion of health. For instance, alcoholics can feel that they are in control and that their problems are minimal. Such a sense of power can even convince them to falsely assume that they can manage as well or better with drinking than without it. Under the influence of alcohol, some people feel that they are more confident, freer, and assertive. Others feel that they are more imaginative, spontaneous, and creative. And indeed some alcoholics manifest these qualities, but negative consequences eventually outweigh and impede positive ones.

Alcohol can also serve to numb one's conscience so that some alcoholics "feel freer" to act in ways that are normally forbidden. Actually, alcohol engenders license (more than freedom) to act the way one wants. For example, alcohol enables some emotionally repressed people to express anger. Such license can be especially destructive when a person has built a slush fund of anger which is then suddenly and intensely expressed under the influence of alcohol.

Alcohol may serve as a catalyst to express other feelings that are normally controlled or repressed. Loneliness, worthlessness, shame, sexuality, envy, jealousy, or practically any feeling may be expressed with alcoholic encouragement. However, such alcoholic expression also involves nonsense. Processing feelings is impeded, and negative feelings can be strengthened. The causes of feelings are seldom ascertained, others may be abused, guilt and shame can emerge or be increased, and alcoholics themselves can be abused. Actually true freedom and health are usually impeded or violated more than fostered.

Drinking alcohol is a legal and accessible way to reduce stress and pain, and in some respects it works insofar as it temporarily reduces discomfort. Alcohol medicates the vulnerability of feeling afraid, the oppression of guilt, the uncertainty of anxiety, and the toxicity of shame. It silences obsessions, reduces compulsive yearnings, slows hyperactivity, lessens intensity, and soothes low self-esteem. Such alcoholic relief is temporary, while true serenity is absent.

In some sense, drinking can be used to nourish oneself. Angela used alcohol in this way. "I have always been a hyper-responsible person. I not only took care of my duties at work and at home, but I also took care of my family's needs, often way beyond the call of duty. But who cared for me? Usually no one. So when the day was over, the kids were in bed, and my husband and mother seemed to be satisfied, I treated myself to some drinks. Looking back, this was the only time I took just for me. It was my misguided attempt to care for myself. Since becoming sober, I have found better ways to love myself — ways that help me to function better."

Most alcoholics enjoy themselves when drinking. And indeed, drinking can be fun and is often associated with enjoyable and memorable times. It is unwise to minimize the sense of drinking; it has a lot going for it. Otherwise, abstinence and sobriety would be easy to achieve. In fact, when alcoholics are in the initial stages of recovery, one of their most difficult tasks is to learn to relax and have fun without alcohol. Without alcohol, many alcoholics feel and think that life is boring or at least drab. To compound this difficulty, the mass media reinforce the connection between fun and "real living" with alcohol.

Alcohol can also engender an experience of pseudo ecstasy. ("Ecstasy" literally means "to stand out" of the ordinary world.) Instead of feeling uptight or perfectionistic, alcohol can bring relaxed and carefree feelings. "Thinkaholics" — people who obsess, intellectualize, or generally live out of their mind — can turn off their mind and rest. Workaholics may use alcohol to move relatively quickly and easily from their ordinary stressful life to relaxation. Indeed, alcoholic workaholics may not know how to relax in any way except with alcohol.

When drinking, alcoholics feel as if they are in a different world where they are no longer bothered with everyday demands — a world of comfort and carefreeness. The relaxed and telltale smile of people who drink too much often indicates such a state. Alcoholics yearn to be in a place where there is perpetual peace. So, many constantly chase the perfect state of ecstasy.

Alcohol offers a feeling of intimacy — a feeling of being with or at least not against reality. Without their fears and other inhibitions, some alcoholics feel more secure and able to risk sharing. Many alcoholics feel less judgmental and more accepting of themselves. Still others feel that they experience a certain presence of God. These and other modes of alcoholic intimacy are meaningful; however, they are likely to be less free, reciprocal, and lasting than sober and healthy intimacy.

So if there are gains, why not drink? The simplest answer is that these so-called positive gains are temporary and fail to foster ongoing healthy growth. They tend to be short term gains that lead to long term losses. The reality is that these "positive" gains are followed and outweighed by negative consequences. Once again, when there are more negative than positive consequences to self and others, alcoholism is present. To become sober, alcoholic sense must be replaced with sober sense, and understanding the following negative consequences can help alcoholics achieve this goal.

Negative Consequences

One of the more obvious consequences is the hangover. Rather than undergoing intense headaches, shakiness, cravings to drink, and an overall feeling of dysfunctionality, one suffers from a normal headache. Soon, perhaps with aspirin, they feel back to "normal." Still, their hangover is a symptom of self-abuse.

Harry describes some of his experiences of drinking alcoholically. "Although I never missed a day of work, I always felt somewhat hungover. My worst day was on a Monday after a weekend of heavier drinking. Then I really felt in a bag. It was as if I had to use energy to do what I should normally do automatically. And although I could recall what happened the previous night, many of my memories were foggy.

"I know now that I didn't function nearly as well as I do now without drinking. Now I get up without a headache, more rested and alert. In general, my work and life are easier and better. Yet, I have to admit that sometimes I'm still tempted to drink to relax, but I know that I'm better off without drinking."

Feeling tired is a common consequence. Even though some alcoholics have a high energy level, their energy is never as great and efficient as it could be without alcohol. Being a depressant, alcohol simply takes its toll. It works on alcoholics, pulls them down, preoccupies them, demands their attention, takes their time and energy. The effects of alcoholism are an extra and unnecessary burden to carry.

Everyday functions, like sleeping and eating, can be impaired. Alcoholics may sleep more than normal, often falling asleep while drinking. Others have disruptive sleep, like waking periodically throughout the night or having a disruptive dream life. Many alcoholics do not eat properly and regularly, or they often drink before or instead of eating. And of course, alcohol "works" more quickly on an empty stomach. Consequently, without proper rest and nourishment, their physical health is impaired.

Alcoholics who are prone to live sedentary lives tend to gain weight. Some, however, follow exercise programs that enable them to stay in relatively good condition as well as cope with their drinking. Although their physical conditioning tends to compensate for some of their abusive drinking, they still are likely to deceive themselves, for they can never be in as good shape as they could without alcohol.

Listen to Jake. "I could never understand why I was always so tired. I worked out in the health club three times a week and ran three other days. I was almost as addicted to exercise as I was to beer. But after working out, I would hit the bar for a couple of happy hours and then go home for a few brews. My weight was low and my muscle tone was better than average, but I was really not in as good a shape as I looked. My eating habits were poor, drinking was preferred to eating, and sleep was restless. I tried to live a normal life in an abnormal way."

Abstract thinking and short-term memory can be impaired. It is as if normal alcoholics can think well as long as they stay within their framework, but when they have to think about and/

or listen to something new, they may have some difficulty processing the new material. These alcoholics often manage this subtle impairment by speaking about and doing what they know and want. In short, they control the situation.

Alcoholics are skilled at compensating and/or covering their impairments of attention, memory, and thinking. When asked questions about the previous night, they speak extensively about what they can recall; thus, they keep control of the situation and put on a good show. To the average person, this looks perfectly normal. But if you live with such an alcoholic, you begin to feel the gaps and lacks.

Such cognitive impairment is exemplified by Sarah's account of her retaking a driver's test because of too many speeding violations. "Thinking I was clever, I got the driving manual and studied for the test while drinking. When I took the test, I had a slight hangover. But what the heck, I thought, I knew all these rules anyhow, and this would be a piece of cake. So I went to take the test with arrogance and incompetence.

"In short, I failed a simple multiple choice test that any high school student could pass. Although I had been driving for 25 years, I failed the exam. Consequently, I had to return to take the written exam again. (Ironically, when I eventually took the driving test, I passed it, for it didn't rely on thinking but rather on automatic habits.)

"The second time I was sure I would pass, and besides, I was mortally embarrassed for having to retake it. Again, I was not drunk, but was drinking my normal second scotch and soda while studying. Why make this more difficult than need be, I thought; I would relax while studying. Furthermore, I knew how to drive. Well, I failed the test a second time.

"Then I really became somewhat panicky, for if I failed a third time, I would lose my license until I was eligible to take the test again. I was so scared that I studied without drinking so that I would be clear when I took the test. Thank God and a little sober sense, I finally passed the test.

"Looking back soberly, I know that the test was relatively easy, and I know that I failed the test because I studied while drinking and took the test with arrogance and cognitive impairment. In fine alcoholic style, I fooled myself into thinking that I could pass the test while drinking, for I knew that some of my alcoholic friends did pass their test while drinking. I guess passing while drinking would have been another way to prove to myself that I was not alcoholic. Even when I did pass, I didn't consciously link my success to being temporarily dry. Crazy? You bet. That's what happens when you're in an alcoholic fog."

The emotional life of alcoholics can take many directions. Emotions can be put on hold in that they are frozen or numbed. Or license may be given to emotional expression so that one becomes explosive and/or weepy. And, some alcoholics simply become mellow but unavailable.

We have seen that many alcoholics are apt to drink to feel more comfortable and experience less pain. Although such tranquilization is human and understandable, it also impedes learning from one's feelings and it harms interpersonal relationships. For instance, rather than sharing, many alcoholics hold in and/or numb their feelings so that others really do not know how they think or feel. Likewise, explosiveness or narcissistic gushing impedes healthy intimacy.

Listen to this woman: "When I got hurt, particularly when I felt that my husband put me down or didn't understand me, I would drink. What increased my pain is that he was in his own world, and he left me in mine. When I sobered up, the pain of his not caring hurt me and perhaps in my mind enabled me to drink even more. Not only was I not dealing with my husband, but more importantly, I was out of touch with myself, which pressured me to drink even more. Thus, I was caught up in a vicious circle.

"Every once in a while, about once or twice a month, I would explode. I know now that I was building up anger that eventually had to explode or implode. I would argue with and scream at my husband, and when he screamed, I would scream more. At other times, he would just leave the house and go out with his friends. Then I would find myself screaming at my kids, who were innocent and had little to do with my anger. And when I would sober up, with a hangover, I felt terribly guilty and ashamed. Instead of listening to my feelings, I would sooner than later alcoholize them again. So I was once again on the alcoholic merry-go-round."

Some people rarely if ever express feelings unless they are under the influence of alcohol. Alcohol lessens their inhibitions, enabling them to express their feelings, albeit "drugged feelings." However, when they do express their feelings, their behavior is often too intense and inappropriate. These alcoholics may justify such extreme expressions by saying, "That's how I feel," or, "I'm just being honest." Nevertheless, such "honest" expression of feeling is often narcissistic or a cover for deeper feelings. And it never justifies violation of other people's well-being.

People who repress feelings and consequently build a slush fund of affectivity are especially vulnerable to alcohol. When they drink alcoholically, their affective dam may break. A normally mild mannered but repressed man may become explosively angry under the influence of alcohol, and his enabler may blame the alcohol rather than focusing on him. Or, a sexually repressed woman who has her drink spiked may behave radically different than her normal self.

Other alcoholics become weepy or express feelings excessively. It is as if they regress to a childish stage that seeks comfort, understanding, and sympathy. Some play the martyr role, feeling that being so persecuted they have the right to drink. Or they may apologize with the rider that they only drink to endure their painful life. Although such drinking can evoke sympathy, it is often manipulative.

Other alcoholics simply drink, mellow out, and fall asleep. Although they seldom directly harm anyone, their lack of cognitive and emotional presence violates and disrupts others. Their absence engenders irresponsibility, inconsistency, unreliability, and unaccountability. Important experiences of intimacy like play, sharing, prayer, and love are at best less than what is appropriate. Since such experiences are necessary for communal and personal health, alcoholics and their loved ones suffer needlessly.

Actually, alcohol more or less affects all aspects of life. Alcohol is a drug that can initially lessen inhibitions and give a sense of liberation, but rather quickly it acts as a depressant that impairs and numbs physical, cognitive, affective, social, and spiritual functions.

Nevertheless, normal alcoholics may function as well as or better than their peers in the public and work-a-day world. When they operate in these functional domains, negative consequences seldom evoke attention, let alone intervention. As long as alcoholics do their jobs and/or function without disrupting others, they are treated as normal.

Some alcoholics feel that they can work better when under the influence of alcohol. For example, some writers and performers feel that they are more effective with alcohol. It is difficult to determine with certainty whether or not these statements are true, but it is fairly safe to say that generally people function better without alcohol. It is a simple and empirical fact that alcohol impedes cognitive and affective functions.

On the other hand, as we have seen, alcohol may reduce inhibitions that can release some creative vision. The difficulty, however, is that people have difficulty implementing their creative insights. In short, although some alcoholics may function well while drinking, they would probably function and work better when sober.

Play and leisure are also effected by alcohol. Some people contend that, when drinking, they have a better time and feel freer to express themselves as well as relate to others. Indeed, although alcohol can engender creative expression, such functions as judgment, control, and visual-motor coordination are impaired. Furthermore, people can learn to be authentically free without alcohol so that their expressiveness and playfulness come from within themselves rather than from alcohol. Listen to Harry's transition from alcoholic to sober playfulness.

"I was always the center of attention at parties, particularly weddings. I would never get rip-roaring drunk, but drank enough to have a pretty steady buzz during the entire festivity. I would sing, dance, and in general cut up — and everybody would want to dance and sing with me. I simply had a good time and everyone had a good time with me.

"When I stopped drinking and got sober, I still went to weddings and parties and had a good time. I still danced, sang, joked, and in general had fun with everyone. The interesting thing was that everyone felt I was still drinking and half drunk, and yet I was cold sober. People automatically assumed that since I was spontaneous and free that I was necessarily drinking. When I told people that I had not had a drop, they thought I was kidding. In fact, people would say, 'Harry, you better slow down; I think you've had too much to drink!'"

Alcoholic fun is not truly free, for the consequences are negative and the likelihood to hurt or be hurt is greater. Furthermore, alcoholic fun tends to be more self-centered than interpersonal. Sober fun, on the other hand, is freer, its consequences last longer, and is more reciprocal as well as respectful to self and others.

Likewise, alcoholic socialization differs from sober socialization. Some people, such as those with low self-esteem or severe self-consciousness, find it difficult to interact without the props of alcohol. It is as if they get their confidence from a bottle. Alcohol numbs or at least lowers their self-consciousness so they feel freer and more confident. In contrast, sober socialization is born out of and increases self-confidence. Being sober, persons express themselves more openly and clearly, are freer and less likely to get into alcoholic trouble, and can manage more effectively.

Indeed, negative effects are seen more clearly and felt more intensely in personal realms like family, marriage, and friendship. Although normal alcoholics can succeed quite well, be well liked, and have positions of social prominence, they can also experience serious disorders in their personal life. Rarely is an alcoholic's marriage healthy.

Interpersonal relations, particularly intimacy, are most adversely affected by alcohol. Because alcohol is a depressant and induces self-absorption, interpersonal relationships are impeded. Self-disclosure and sharing are altered through an alcoholic persona. Although alcohol can initially lessen inhibitions, we have seen that such freedom is largely an illusion. And when both persons are drinking, self and mutual deception as well as other negative effects can be denied or easily pushed aside.

Imagine you are sober and trying to be intimate with someone who is drinking. You experience impediments such as alcoholic odors and subtle visual motor impairments as well as the drinking person's being less than fully present to you. Keep in mind that presence is not a matter of all or nothing. The alcoholic may indeed be present — touching and touchable, listening and speaking, loving and lovable, but there are alcoholic impediments and frustrations. Although you may try to give fully of yourself, the alcoholic is unable to do so. Consequently, the relationship is not as reciprocal as it can be, and can be frustratingly unequal.

To be sure, alcoholics can be and often are intimate and good people. Nevertheless, whether the alcoholic be a pleaser, a withdrawn and avoidant person, an aggressor, a controller, or whatever, intimacy suffers. In short, interpersonal relationships and intimacy do not work as well with alcohol as they do with sobriety.

When intimacy suffers, one's whole life suffers. Without intimacy nothing makes consistent and permanent sense. This is not to say that a person needs to be married or in love with a particular person on an ongoing basis. It simply means that one must develop intimacy with oneself, with people, with life, and with a Higher Power in order to lead a meaningful, free, and healthy life. Authentic intimacy is the heartbeat of healthiness.

Self intimacy is also violated. Alcohol anesthetizes uncomfortable feelings and eventually exacerbates their pain. The more alcoholics drink, the lonelier, more anxious, and depressed they eventually get. Relief is temporary and is soon replaced with long-term, misery. Alcoholics act as if they are trying to put out a fire with fuel. They grab a container thinking that it is filled with water, but actually it is gasoline. Likewise, in the final analysis, alcohol fuels the painful nonsense of feeling and extinguishes the sense.

Alcohol can be a lover that deepens and widens the hole in one's heart. For instance, loneliness can be numbed but not taken away by alcohol; only love is an adequate answer to the questions of loneliness. And although the discomfort of anxiety can be lessened with alcohol, its source is not dealt with; consequently, anxiety will reemerge, often stronger than ever. One can cope with boredom through alcohol, but boredom like the other feelings returns. While alcohol may take away the anxious emptiness and helplessness of depression, alcohol itself is a depressant and only increases overall depression. So, although there may be temporary relief, such uncomfortable feelings only increase rather than decrease. To repeat: the challenge is to listen to the message of these uncomfortable feelings and respond to them in more effective ways. Alcohol resolves nothing.

The relationship between alcohol and spirituality is especially interesting and seductive as indicated by the etymological meaning of alcohol — spirit. Consider that alcohol can break down ego boundaries that constrict experiences of God, lessen fears that impede spiritual experiences, and open one to trans-rational experiences. When ego and superego impediments are weakened, one can be more open to spiritual experiences. On the other hand, such experiences are contaminated with and by alcohol. Alcohol also impedes the positive consequences of spiritual experiences so that they have less of an effect on one's every day behavior. Reflect on the experience of this alcoholic monk who has a Ph.D. in spirituality.

"God, did I fool myself when I was drinking. I actually convinced myself that drinking helped my spiritual growth. But looking back on my experience, it is understandable.

"One of my alcoholic sojourns was to follow a kind of ritual several times a week. In the evenings, I would drink until I reached a pleasant high, and then I would light a candle and say some prayers. I felt I was truly being one with God. And perhaps, I was. I sort of drifted off to a semi-conscious state where I felt one with reality, a pleasant sense of contented oneness. I no longer felt at odds and alienated like I normally did during the day. Understandably, I looked forward to these times. In theory, I know that I should try to achieve this experience without alcohol, but it felt kind of natural or at least easier this way.

"After about three years of sober living, I learned to have contemplative experiences without alcohol. For me, it is interesting to reflect on the similarities and differences between my sober and alcoholic spiritual experiences. In both I felt one with reality — that is, I experienced a "being with" rather than "being against" or a stressful coping with reality. I experienced an inner harmony wherein problems subsided or at least were not so problematic, and life took on a broader and deeper perspective.

"Nevertheless, there were some definite and important differences between my sober and semi-drunk experiences. One difference was that my alcoholic spiritual experiences did not seem to last, or they did not seem to carry over into my everyday life. For instance, the next morning I know that I had a good experience, but I had difficulty retrieving it. I felt that it made some difference, but I did not know how or what difference. It was as if the experience was always just beyond my grasp or an experience that made sense but I didn't know what sense.

"Being sober, I can reflect on my spiritual experiences and see how they are practically effective and helpful in my everyday life. When under stress or not, I know that God is with me, and this realization helps me to cope better. I guess what I'm saying is that the pragmatic effects of sober spirituality are much greater than alcoholic spirituality. It seemed like alcohol spirituality was only for the moment and that sober spirituality has long-term effects.

"I also feel much freer in being sober and spiritual. I no longer have to depend on alcohol to experience God's Presence, but I have many more approaches such as meditation, contemplation, centering prayer, appreciating God's Presence in the ordinary, and experiencing the community of God, self, and others. And of course, I don't have the hangover from my so-called alcoholic spirituality.

"Furthermore, the experience itself is clear rather than through a fog. When I was drinking, my spiritual experiences were misty and not nearly as present as they are now. To paraphrase that song from *Godspell*, I experience God more clearly, dearly, and nearly. I guess I'm saying that I'm more frequently and freely present to God sober than I was when I was drinking."

Drinking may indeed help to break down ego and superego impediments that may enable spiritual experiences to occur; such impediments, however, can be worked through more freely without alcohol. To practice sober discipline in terms of meditative and contemplative procedures such as using a mantra or centering prayer engenders freer and healthier spiritual experiences. And as the monk mentioned, the consequences last, impact more effectively on everyday living, and promote freedom and serenity.

Although alcoholics can live spiritually, they are in constant conflict because alcohol demands to be a replacement for God. By definition, alcoholism means that God is displaced as the center of life. Alcohol becomes the saving grace.

To conclude: It is critical to recovery to admit to both the positive and negative consequences of alcoholism. Sobriety entails accepting the loss of alcoholic sense and replacing it with

healthy sense. And when alcoholics can reflect on the immediate and long-term negative consequences of drinking, they are
less apt to drink and more likely to maintain and foster sobriety.

6 Diagnosis

The gateway to recovery is admitting to alcoholism. Yet as we have seen, such acceptance is very difficult partly because most alcoholics are more normal than abnormal. Since alcoholism is usually unrecognized and enabled, how do you know if you or another is alcoholic? This chapter deals with ways to increase our awareness of normal alcoholism so we can make responsible decisions and take necessary action.

Diagnostic Guidelines

The following questions and commentaries offer an overall idea of what constitutes normal alcoholism and will serve as a guideline to discern the presence of alcoholism. Try to respond to the questions honestly and spontaneously. Keep in mind that you need not share the results with anyone but yourself and that your answers are not conclusive proof of a positive diagnosis. Nevertheless, your responses will give you data to reflect on and perhaps encourage you to share your thoughts with a person who is knowledgeable about alcoholism.

1. Do you feel good about controlling your drinking and/or abstinence?
2. Do others say that you are a better or nicer person when you are not drinking?

3. Do you miss drinking when you quit for awhile?
4. Do you feel proud about never having caused or gotten into serious trouble on account of your drinking?
5. Do you act differently when drinking?
6. Do fun and drinking go together?
7. Is it a sacrifice to abstain from drinking at festive occasions?
8. Do nondrinkers seem odd?
9. Do you feel more comfortable when drinking?
10. Do you savor the way you feel when you drink?
11. Do you have hangovers?
12. Do you feel that you might have a drinking problem or that you tend to drink too much?
13. Do you usually function well when drinking?
14. Do you sometimes stop drinking?
15. Are many of your friends drinkers?
16. Does alcohol help you to cope?
17. Do you seldom lose control when drinking?
18. Do you drink too much and too often?
19. Do you drink secretively?
20. Do you justify your drinking?
21. Does your drinking cause more harm than good to yourself and others?
22. When you stop drinking, do you feel more anxious than usual?

A yes response to more than one of these questions should be a matter of concern; more than three positive responses indicates alcoholic drinking; and if you agree with more than six of these questions, you probably are an alcoholic. If you have any doubt about your drinking, it would behoove you to share your drinking problem with an expert and/or a recovering alcoholic. Whatever you do, reflect on these questions.

1. *Do you feel good about controlling your drinking and/or abstinence?* This question may initially sound nonsensical or contradictory, for one might assume that people feel good about con-

trol and abstinence. Yet, think about it. Nondrinkers or nonalcoholic drinkers rarely give control or abstinence a thought. When they do drink too much, they recognize and take responsibility for their behavior. For them, abstinence comes naturally rather than as a task to be achieved.

Alcoholics feel that it is a big deal when they control their drinking or abstain for a long period of time. Bragging about abstinence is often an attempt to justify themselves. Actually, such boasting indicates the likelihood of a drinking problem. Unlike non-alcoholics, alcoholics tend to obsess about their success, and their very obsessiveness about succeeding is an indicator of alcoholism.

Listen to Harriet. "I was never a full blown alcoholic, but rather a polished, sophisticated one. I managed to hold down a middle management job as well as doing a pretty good job in raising three kids. I seldom if ever drank when I had responsibilities at work or home. Most of my drinking was during the evenings after everything had settled down and everyone was in bed. I was proud of being successful in both my professional and personal lives, which somehow proved that I was not an alcoholic.

"Although my husband drank, he didn't the way I did. When we would go to dinner and the theater, he might have a drink or two; whereas, I would normally have three or more. More importantly, drinking didn't seem to be important to him. He simply didn't look at or think about drinking like I did.

"Despite getting a bit high, I always managed to function well, never embarrassing myself. Nevertheless, my husband on several occasions did voice his concern about my drinking. Of course, my contentious counter attack was to point out to him that I never lost a day's work, that I functioned as good or better than he, and that I would frequently quit drinking. But after a few weeks or longer, I would return to my normal drinking pattern. Or when we would go to a wedding or some such celebration, I never drank. Thus, my husband as well as others could see that I did not look and act like an alcoholic."

2. *Do others say that you are a better or a nicer person when you are not drinking?* Never underestimate the feedback that you get from others. When people, particularly those who live with you, complain about you, seldom are they speaking pure nonsense. Even in the midst of their critical speech, there is usually much truth. For instance, when people say that you are easier to get along with when you are not drinking, they are usually making an important statement. However, because of denial, collusion, and continued alcoholic drinking, alcoholics have difficulty listening to anything that threatens their drinking.

Try to listen to why people think that you are a better person when you are not drinking. As in other matters, value their opinion. Listen to your spouse, children, parents, friends, brothers and sisters; then verbalize what you hear as honestly as you can. Ask yourself if you are really better off drinking instead of not drinking.

Remember: Alcoholics are not good judges of their drinking, and they are very protective of their drinking. They are likely to minimize the harm they are doing to self and others and to maximize the positive. It behooves alcoholics to think of how much they may be harming others and self by their absence, by their lack of enjoyment with others, by their overall avoidance, by their control of others especially in their family.

Harry describes his inability to listen to the truth of his wife's comments. "I hated it when my wife said that she liked me better when I was sober. When I wasn't drinking, she said, I was more sensitive and reliable. And when I was drinking, I tended to be unreliable, in my own world, and moody. My wife often said that she found it difficult to relax when I was drinking because she never knew what to expect next. Her complaints made little sense to me. How and the hell could she feel so miserable when I felt so good?

"Only after I was sober for a good year did I begin to realize the truth in what my wife had been saying. It seemed that her critical remarks always threatened me and made me angry, but now I can see the truth in what she said. Actually, when she learned to give detached and compassionate feedback, she was much more effective than when she bitched desperately and incessantly.

"I now know what my wife meant when she complained about my not really caring. I feel deep regret for how I treated my family, even though I was never explicitly violent or abusive to them. I feel the best way that I can make amends is by living a good sober life, by really caring."

3. *Do you miss drinking when you quit for awhile?* When on the wagon, that is, not drinking but not necessarily sober, alcoholics feel that something important is missing in their lives. Once again, they often feel cheated, that they are making a sacrifice, or that something is absent which really should be present. They feel a nagging void in their lives without drinking. To think about not drinking forever is depressing and frightening.

When healthy people have the opportunity to drink, they either have a drink or abstain, and rarely give it a second thought. In contrast, alcoholic drinkers think about drinking when they are not drinking. In a sense, drinking is present in its absence. Alcoholics may go for days without giving drinking a thought, but sooner than later the voice of drinking lures them. It is as if they are trying to end a passionate love affair, while periodically and consistently yearning for their lover.

Consider normal people at a celebration: They may or may not have a drink; in fact, they are not very concerned about drinking. Alcoholics, however, have to work at not drinking. Even the sight of people drinking may bother them. Alcoholics feel that they are missing something important when they are not drinking.

"Every Lent I would quit drinking," says Alice. "And practically every day I would think of Easter Saturday when the official time of Lent ended, for then I could drink again. It is not that I suffered withdrawal symptoms; in fact, quitting during Lent was relatively easy. But the thought that I could and would go back to drinking was always more or less on my mind.

"In short, I looked forward to Easter not so much because of the Resurrection of Christ, but more because of the resurrection of my drinking. It was like I had a void in me that I learned to tolerate and endure in service of a Lenten repentance. I felt that I was temporarily dead, and when I drank on Easter, I felt alive again."

If the thought of permanent abstinence scares you, even though you may function well without alcohol, you may be alcoholic. If happiness necessarily includes alcohol, you are probably an alcoholic.

4. *Do you feel proud about never having caused or gotten into serious trouble?* Most alcoholics are careful when and where they drink. For instance, they exercise controlled public drinking which lessens the likelihood of getting into social and legal difficulty. Or they manage to drink and look normal so that no one questions their sobriety. They take pride in such accomplishments.

John expresses this self-deception in the following manner. "When I was drinking, I always felt a relief about not causing any difficulty or getting into trouble. But when I look back on my drinking days, God had to have been with me. It amazes me that I didn't have an accident or at least be stopped by the police the many times I drove while less than sober. Socially, I always managed to back off or avoid trouble. I felt a certain pride about this. Surely, someone who can control themselves so much is not an alcoholic, I rationalized. Now that I am sober, I simply no longer experience this feeling of relief, for I have nothing to worry about. Furthermore, I am less proud and more humble."

5. *Do you act differently when drinking?* Anyone who drinks too much will more or less act differently. And if you drink too much too often, you are probably problematic and alcoholic. Some alcoholics become aggressive or oppositional; others be-

come pleasing and co-dependent, and others simply avoid and isolate. Whatever the style, drinking induces one to act more or less differently than he or she would act in a sober state. And if you like the alcoholic difference, you will seek it.

This woman acted differently and liked it. "I still miss my drinking days. When I drank, I became aggressive, particularly toward arrogant and chauvinistic people. I liked being a feisty bitch, and others seemed to like it too, except for those who felt my wrath.

"My so-called freedom was in stark contrast to my dry self who was angry but ignorant about how to express it. Drinking helped me come out of my shy and withdrawn self. When drinking, I could really express how I felt and thought. Now I am learning without the crutch to be assertive rather than aggressive. I have to admit that it is more difficult, but I know it is better because I am in control, not at the mercy of Mr. Beefeater. I am learning to be truly free."

6. *Do fun and drinking go together?* Alcoholics of whatever type find it very difficult to have fun without alcohol. When alcoholics begin to get sober, many find it difficult to learn to enjoy themselves and others without drinking. Or they have fun but not nearly as much as they did when drinking.

If you cannot have as much fun without drinking as you do when drinking, you may be alcoholic. Such a statement can sound extreme to somebody who is alcoholic. It simply does not make sense to an alcoholic to have more fun sober than when drinking. To have fun is to drink.

Sarah expresses one of the many scenarios of this theme. "When I was drinking, I couldn't imagine going on vacation without drinking. It didn't seem right. To go to the beach without alcohol didn't make sense. It felt wrong. In fact, I got anxious thinking about it. What would I do during happy hours? How could I go to dinner without drinking? A vacation without alcohol scared me and felt depressing.

"Anyhow, to make the story short, I found that the so-called impossible was possible. In many respects, the anticipation of leisure without alcohol was worse than the reality. Once I really tried having fun with sobriety, I found that it got progressively better and easier. To be honest, however, I still occasionally miss those carefree, painless, high, alcoholic days. But overall, I'm much better off. And guess what? Vacations are possible and even better with sobriety."

Very often alcoholics have grown up in alcoholic family systems that associated festive times with drinking. Since holidays and special celebrations always included considerable alcohol when they were children, alcoholics observed the model of enjoyment and drinking going together. Learning through observation reinforced them to have unrealistic expectations — that fun must include drinking. Or, if they enjoy themselves without drinking, they feel it is not as good as enjoyment with drinking.

One of the more difficult passages in recovery is to learn to have fun without drinking. Just to be dry is only part of the story. True sobriety presupposes being dry (not drinking) and also learning to enjoy life. One common reason dry alcoholics are miserable is that they have not learned to enjoy themselves without drinking.

After the initial stages of being dry, many alcoholics find themselves in a vacuum — a nowhere land between previous drinking and not yet being sober. Since this "in-between" time evokes anxiety and uncertainty, it is very important to learn to fill the void with healthy experiences. For instance, one of the many functions of A.A. is that it provides recovering alcoholics healthy ways to enjoy themselves without drinking. Although A.A. is basically a spiritual program for recovery, it also responds to recreational and social needs as well.

If you have difficulty having fun or feel anxious about drinking in a recreational situation, it is a sign that you are an alcoholic. For alcoholics, life without alcohol is boring. Sober drinkers enjoy themselves with or without a drink; their enjoyment does not necessarily include or depend on alcohol.

7. *Is it a sacrifice to abstain from drinking at festive occasions?* This question affirms the preceding recurrent theme: Alcoholics need alcohol to have fun, to relax, to be content, to celebrate. When alcoholics go to a festive occasion like a wedding, they look forward to drinking. In fact, to go to a wedding reception that has no alcohol would seem ridiculous or "not normal" to them. Not to drink at a festive occasion sounds to them like a contradiction in terms. Healthy people shrug their shoulders with indifference. Or, they might think that it is a little different, but unlike the alcoholic it is no sacrifice for them to go to such a reception. If you find yourself disgruntled or expending your energy preparing yourself for a celebration without alcohol, you are probably alcoholic. To feel incomplete without alcohol at festive occasions indicates alcoholic issues.

Another variation of this theme is that many alcoholics look forward to drinking during holidays. Abstinence during a holiday like New Year's is absurd or at least is felt to be unfair or abnormal. Again, for alcoholics, holidays and drinking go together; one without the other makes sad sense. During the holidays, they look forward to the punch bowl, to the champagne, to the gin and tonic, to the hot toddy, to the shot and beer, to whatever alcohol they prefer.

Some families center their holiday gatherings around alcohol. As soon as you enter their house, you are offered a drink. And if you refuse, you get a frown or a question about what is wrong. To refuse a drink in an alcoholic family system is almost insulting. To gather around a bottle of cheer during the holidays is something that is expected and cherished. To get close and to feel the holiday warmth, the good will, and cheer without the cheer of alcohol seem unthinkable.

8. *Do nondrinkers seem odd?* Alcoholics look at nondrinkers with some amazement and bewilderment, particularly if these nondrinkers were alcoholic. Alcoholics may know theoretically that it is possible to live well without drinking, but experientially

nondrinkers baffle them. They simply have a difficult time putting themselves in the nondrinkers place.

This difficulty in understanding is often evident when alcoholics become sober and meet with actively alcoholic friends. Alcoholic friends will look at recovering alcoholics as odd. A recovering person is likely to hear statements like: "Aren't you drinking anymore, what's wrong?" "Are you sick?" Rarely does the recovering person hear statements like: "It's really good to see that you are not drinking." "I can appreciate your becoming sober." "I'm happy for you. I think its great that you are no longer drinking." "I wish I could follow your example." If you feel nondrinkers are odd, difficult to understand, sad, or sick, you are probably an alcoholic and/or co-alcoholic.

9. *Do you feel more comfortable when drinking?* Alcoholics, relatively functional or dysfunctional, feel more at ease and content when drinking. In many respects, contentment is the primary reason for drinking; without such an immediate gain drinking alcoholically makes little sense. Alcoholics do not drink primarily for the taste or to quench their thirst. More likely, alcoholics drink to satisfy a craving, to numb uncomfortable feelings, lessen inhibitions, elicit aggression, encourage confidence and sociability, engender mellowness and sedation, etc. — all more or less in service of being more comfortable. A challenge for recovering alcoholics is to be comfortable and content without alcohol.

To yearn for a drink because it offers you the certainty of contentment makes sense, albeit not recommended sense. You know you can depend on alcohol to give you what you want. Unlike interpersonal relationships or other activities, drinking alcoholically involves relatively little time, energy, effort, risk, or vulnerability — and its effect is almost guaranteed. Feeling more comfortable when drinking is understandable and is probably alcoholic.

"I always felt more comfortable when I drank and without

alcohol I felt uneasy, less secure, somehow not quite right," explains Fran. "Being at a ball game without booze didn't feel right. Or not drinking a few beers after work felt like something was missing. Without my beer, I got jumpy — like I was out of sorts. It was no big deal to go without drinking, but why make life more difficult, I reasoned. Life is tough enough, so if I can make it better, why not have a few beers? There is nothing wrong with that, is there?"

The issue is not what is "right or wrong," but it is more a matter of what is healthy. To depend on alcohol as your primary way to relax or function more comfortably is not healthy. Alcohol is a biochemical depressant that impedes true freedom. Other less dependent ways to achieve contentment and especially serenity are available. In the short run, however, sober ways may not be as easy and available as alcohol, but in the long run their effects last much longer and are healthier for self and others.

Since alcohol is a main source of comfort and support, alcoholics yearn to be with alcohol. They can rely on alcohol, predict with some certainty its effect, and feel safe with alcohol. Unlike involvement with persons, they need not risk rejection or that the outcome will be different from what they expect. In fact, in the early and middle stages of alcoholism alcohol can be relied on as a trusted friend. The bottle has a lot going for it.

So, if you frequently drink to relax or be content, you are probably alcoholic. Healthy non-alcoholics learn to relax without drinking as well as to accept and deal with their discontent. Alcoholics need alcohol to cope and nourish themselves.

10. *Do you savor the way you feel when you drink?* Normal people, who occasionally drink, make no big deal out of it. And when normal persons drink too much, they accept their behavior and rarely if ever overdrink again. Normal persons are heard to say things like: "I'm not going to drink like that again for a long time." "No way, the way I felt the next morning is not worth it." "I don't like feeling out of control." "I just don't like drink-

ing very much. It makes me feel anxious." And they back up their words with sober behavior. Normal persons have a different experience of alcohol. Rather than savoring alcohol, they easily ignore it.

Indeed, alcoholics like very much the way that they feel when they drink — feelings of contentment, of things coming together, the experience of serenity, the buzz that they try to maintain. If alcoholics did not savor drinking, it would be much easier to quit and become sober. And their negative consequences are not experienced as great enough to outweigh the pleasantness of drinking. Why quit if you can manage well, be relatively successful, and feel relaxed through drinking? Why give up something that you can depend on to make you feel content?

11. *Do you have hangovers?* We have seen that hangovers in normal alcoholics are usually not drastic ones, but rather more subtle and less dysfunctional. Hangovers, for example, are more likely to include slight rather than severe headaches, a mild feeling of being beat rather than severe fatigue, mild difficulty with visual-motor coordination, etc. Thus, it is easier to deceive oneself as well as others in regard to negative consequences, and in this case: the hangover. Such alcoholics can easily rationalize, minimize, or simply deny hangovers that are not grossly disruptive.

With few exceptions, when you drink alcoholically, you are likely to have hangovers. Indeed, there are alcoholics who never or rarely suffer hangovers, at least severe ones. Nevertheless, most alcoholics have at least more than two a year, and not infrequently several per week. Hangovers become a "normal" part of living an alcoholic life. Alcoholics learn to manage them by controlling the amount of drinking thus moderating the severity of their hangovers. Although normal alcoholics suffer hangovers, they do not get out of hand very often or for very long.

12. *Do you feel that you might have a drinking problem or that you tend to drink too much?* A somewhat simplistic but standard

rule is that if you have doubts about being an alcoholic, you probably are one. Such a statement may sound simplistic especially
to alcoholics because they can so easily rationalize and deny their
alcoholic drinking. In contrast to alcoholics, healthy people do
not question their drinking. They simply know that they are not
alcoholic. They rarely give it a thought.

Alcoholics are often bothered cognitively and/or affectively
about their drinking. They wonder about their manner of drinking and why they have to control their drinking. Watching your
drinking habits, trying to appear to be a person who drinks without problems, hiding your drinking, feeling uneasy, and giving
reasons for or "normalizing" your drinking indicate alcoholic
drinking. Again, sober people simply do not go through such
cognitive, affective, and behavioral maneuvers. And, if some
people consider you a heavy drinker, it is a good bet that you are
an alcoholic. Heavy or problem drinking is often a euphemism
for alcoholism. Many people are reluctant to call such people
alcoholic often because they view an alcoholic as being totally
out of control. We have seen that although such a belief is common, it is false.

13. *Do you usually function well when drinking?* This may
sound like an odd or contradictory question, but alcoholics falsely
assume that since they do function well, they are not alcoholic.

Normal alcoholics are in the middle between normal and
dysfunctional drinking: They are normal in that they manage
relatively well, and yet they drink alcoholically. Thus, the deception to self and others partly lies in the fact that they are like
both the normal and the abnormal person. Thus, it may sound
strange to say that if you function well and drink, you may be
alcoholic. In short, functioning well is no proof of the absence
of alcoholism.

This alcoholic managed quite well. "I certainly did not stand
out from the crowd. I was like everybody else, yet I am an alcoholic. One reason that I looked so normal is that I did most of

my drinking between 11:30 and 2:00 a.m. Fortunately or unfortunately, my sales job enabled me to have a flexible schedule so that I could get my sleep. And if I had to rise early, I could usually catch a cat-nap during the day. Anyhow, after my wife went to bed, I started to sedate myself with alcohol. To this day, I don't think she knows how much and how frequently I drank, nor does anyone else.

"I wasn't consciously trying to hide my drinking, but in effect that's what happened. I just liked drinking at the time. It was quiet and nobody was there to bother me. I could do what I wanted — primarily make love to my bottle, which didn't help my love life with my wife. Anyhow, this was the time of the day that I looked forward to — when I could be alone and relax without any disruption. To me, it was a just reward for a hard day's work, and besides, I didn't bother anyone. Oh, how I fooled myself."

14. *Do you sometimes stop drinking?* Most people, whether alcoholic or not, will falsely assume that since they can stop drinking, they are not alcoholic. Actually, the opposite is probably true. Just the fact that you feel you can stop drinking is usually an indicator that you are alcoholic. Non-alcoholics rarely think about abstinence; alcoholics do.

To stop drinking means that you have been drinking. To think about abstaining is an affirmation of a problem of drinking. Indeed, not all alcoholics think extensively about abstinence, but most do. The fact is that thinking about stopping is an indicator that you drink alcoholically. Or, to think of control indicates lack of control.

Such self-deception is succinctly verbalized by Maureen. "Every year after the Super Bowl party, I would stop drinking. Although I drank alcoholically almost every day, I would stay dry until Memorial Day with, of course, the exception of St. Patrick's Day. Such annual abstinence would enable me to lose weight for the summer season, and by Memorial Day I was in shape to begin my extended alcoholic season."

15. *Are many of your friends drinkers?* If most of your friends drink too much and too often, it may mean that you also drink alcoholically. Conversely, non-alcoholics are unlikely to socialize with alcoholics.

As one alcoholic said: "Since I have become sober, I look differently at family reunions. It seems that everybody is in their own world and talking through a fog. I simply don't feel at home anymore, and I feel sad about that. On the other hand, I know that it is best for me not to drink even though I feel out of it when everybody is drinking. Still, I try to accept everyone as they are and seek out the people who are sober. Drunk or sober, they're still my family."

Alcoholics have a difficult time consistently recreating with people who do not drink. To socialize with nondrinkers is burdensome or at least not much fun. People tend to seek their own kind: Drinkers seek drinkers, and nondrinkers seek nondrinkers. Interacting with or without alcohol are simply different experiences. Although alcoholics and non-alcoholics can mix, the mix is not as good as it can be.

16. *Does alcohol help you to cope?* Again, such a question may seem asinine. If alcohol helps one to cope, then how can one be alcoholic? Some alcoholics need and use alcohol in order to function better. They are adept at modulating the amount of alcohol so that they function as well as their peers or at least good enough to get by. Some alcoholics are quite skilled at getting buzzed and at the same time conduct a meeting. Some writers can write well while under the influence of alcohol. Some salespersons seem to do their best when in a slight alcoholic fog. And such functional success is a reinforcement to drink even more.

Healthy drinkers and nondrinkers would rarely if ever think about drinking in order to function better. On rare occasions normal people may drink to feel better but not necessarily to function better. To drink to do a better job does not make sense to the normal person. To some alcoholics, however, drinking and functioning make sense. For them, drinking lessens tension and increases productivity.

17. *Do you seldom lose control when drinking?* Again, alcoholics will reason that if they seldom lose control, they are not alcoholic. For instance, if normal alcoholics hear an A.A. lead that includes serious loss of control, they interpret such a lead as proof they are not alcoholic because they rarely lose control.

A difference between alcoholics and healthy persons is that healthy persons do not take pride in keeping control when they drink. Again: Normal people simply think differently about alcohol. While alcoholics drink too much and take pride in not losing control, healthy persons rarely give this a thought.

18. *Do you drink too much and too often?* This question may be difficult to answer because it demands honesty, and most alcoholics tend to minimize their drinking habits. If you drink too much and too often, you are alcoholic.

Healthy people rarely drink too much, that is: to the point of feeling high or alcoholically content. Such a mild drunk is rare for sober persons, and rather common for alcoholics. Furthermore, healthy people do not drink too often. They can take or leave alcohol. Alcoholics have to take alcohol, and if they leave it, they feel something important is missing.

Harold thought that his drinking was normal — not too much and not too often. When asked about his drinking, he responded: "Not much. You know, just enough to take the edge off. I want to feel relaxed when I get home." With persistent prodding, he proceeded to explain that stopping at his favorite "watering hole" was a daily affair. When asked how much he drank, Harold said, "Oh, you know, just a couple." When pressured to be more specific, he responded with "a few shots and beers," and with more pressure he said: "Oh, I guess about four or five rounds." To Harold his drinking was normal as compared to his alcoholic friends and to his alcoholic family background. But actually,

Harold's drinking is not healthy. It is too much and too often, and is alcoholic.

19. *Do you drink secretively?* If you drink in secret, hide your drinking, or feel embarrassed when discovered, you are probably alcoholic. The aim of such secretive drinking is to give the impression that you have no alcoholic problem, that you are sober. Such secretive drinking often indicates that you may be moving toward more dysfunctional alcoholism and/or that people are beginning to question your drinking.

Sober people do not hide their drinking; they have nothing to hide or feel embarrassed about. When serving drinks, they do not secretly give themselves twice as much as they give others. And when they drink, they drink in public and have no concern about being exposed. Only alcoholics hide their drinking.

Sheila was a very successful mother, daughter, personnel director, and alcoholic. Listen to her: "I have to give myself credit, or perhaps discredit and sympathy. I was real good at hiding my drinking. My two children rarely saw me drinking, and I left my husband because he was a drunk. My parents thought I was super-woman, a perfect lady. I was quite successful professionally and was a model worker.

"But I drank fairly consistently. I almost always drank in private — out of everyone's sight. In public, I would seldom drink, and when I did, I had a maximum of two drinks. When everyone was in bed, however, the story was different. I would drink to get mellow and then sustain this comfortable euphoria until I fell asleep.

"Furthermore, you would never see alcohol in the house except on festive occasions; otherwise, the bottles were hidden. Nobody knew I was alcoholic. God! The time and energy I spent drinking, hiding, and lying was incredible. Thank God, I'm now sober. What a relief!"

To be sure, not all alcoholics are like Sheila. Many drink relatively openly. Often they join other alcoholics, and they reinforce one another. And they frequently live with co-alcoholics who tolerate and enable their alcoholism. They may falsely assume that drinking is their business and that it is not harming anyone. Still, even these alcoholics usually do some "hidden drinking," such as drinking in various situations and with different patterns. Or, some purchase their alcohol at several stores so no one can detect what and how much they drink. In whatever case, these less secretive alcoholics deny or minimize the negative consequences to self and others — a serious type of hiding.

20. *Do you justify your drinking?* Healthy people rarely justify or rationalize their drinking because they do not drink alcoholically. However, alcoholics are apt to perform mental gymnastics to justify their drinking. They make statements like: "I work hard and deserve a reward." "I just take the edge off." "Everyone needs to relax." "This is a shot and beer town. So, when in Rome, do what the Romans do." "Who wouldn't drink with a husband like mine." "It's my life, I'll do what I want." "I'm not hurting anyone." "I'm responsible." "I'm not a drunk." "God understands."

Such justifications are futile attempts to make a negative experience (alcoholic drinking) a positive one. Actually, these rationalizations affirm the existence of a problem in spite of denial. No matter how hard they try to justify their drinking, the fact remains that their drinking is alcoholic.

Listen to these rationalizations. "I would say and do anything to justify my drinking. Of course, this made alcoholic sense because booze was my god — it was my source of comfort, my reprieve, my lover. Since alcohol was my paramount concern, no one was going to take it away. Remember, my rights and well-being (so I thought) were at stake. A life without alcohol didn't make sense. In fact, it scared me.

"One of my main approaches was to admit drinking too much on occasion, but it was no big deal — just being human. Nobody is perfect, I reasoned, and almost everyone sometimes goes to extremes. Look, I said, I don't overeat, oversleep, watch too much television, miss work, skip church, etc. I had to have some fault, and drinking was it. Sure, I drank too much, but I wasn't an alcoholic.

"I humbly but firmly maximized my accomplishments — that I was highly successful in my work, that everyone was pleased — and, I focused on how responsible I was financially, religiously, recreationally. I had an answer for every question. On the other hand, I minimized the negative impact my drinking had on me and especially my family. I focused on the positive and denied the negative. Only when I began to think of the possible impact of my drinking on my family did I begin to consider that I might be an alcoholic."

21. *Does your drinking cause more harm than good to yourself and others?* Again, such a question demands rigorous honesty. Indeed, alcoholics may be honest about other things, but not honest about their drinking. Usually, people who live with an alcoholic are more capable of making an accurate diagnosis.

One of the conclusive indicators of alcoholism is that it causes more negative than positive consequences. With normal alcoholics, however, the untoward effects are subtle; they are usually seen more clearly in the backstage of interpersonal life rather than in the public stage of work. Normal alcoholism specifically impedes intimacy, for it engenders self absorption and a relative lack of personal presence to self and others.

Some alcoholics argue that drinking releases pent-up feelings and enables them to share themselves more openly. Indeed alcohol can initially lessen inhibitions and increase affective expression (while for others alcohol anesthetizes feelings). Such alcoholically induced expression is dependent on alcohol and is far from open and free. Furthermore, alcohol impedes cognitive and volitional processes that conflict with emotional intimacy. Alcohol depresses oneself, depletes energy, and induces self-centeredness in spite of one's best intentions.

Healthy people rarely cause more harm than good by their

drinking. If their drinking does cause harm, they are quick to abstain from drinking for a considerable period of time, and they often make amends. They simply think that it is foolish to pay the price of drinking alcoholically. Alcoholics, on the other hand, minimize and rationalize the negative consequences, or they feel that the benefits of drinking outweigh the negative consequences. Indeed this may feel right to alcoholics, but not to other people.

Remember, since we are not isolated individuals but rather live in an interpersonal network, we impact one another positively and/or negatively. When alcoholics just look at themselves, it is easier to justify their drinking, but when they look beyond themselves at the impact that their drinking has on others, they are more likely to admit that they drink alcoholically. When you can see how your drinking impacts negatively on others, you may re-evaluate your drinking and consider becoming sober.

22. *When you stop drinking do you feel more anxious than usual?* Normal alcoholics, especially in the beginning stages, often drink to lessen anxiety, to engender courage, or simply to have a good time. For instance, some alcoholics drink because of repressed experiences, and when these frightening feelings demand recognition, they drink even more.

Healthy people are more likely to face their problems and seldom numb them with alcohol or other activities like overeating, tranquilizers, and work. So, if you feel extra anxious and frightened when you stop drinking, it is a sign that you have personal issues that should be faced and resolved, and it is a sign that you drink alcoholically.

Carol speaks to this issue: "The first eight months of sobriety were great. As they say, I was in the pink cloud of recovery. Indeed it was a reward for my labors. But then my heavenly bliss began to turn hellish. Initially, I felt vaguely anxious — like I was living in the shadow of a dark cloud. I felt sad, sort of depressed, even angry — a feeling I never allowed. Actually, I was really feeling clearly for the first time since I was a child. What is going on, I wondered.

"Sometimes I felt a passing urge to drink — to numb these uncomfortable feelings. But I knew and largely felt that sobriety was better. And I came to realize that I had always had these feelings, and when they surfaced, I alcoholized them. Now my challenge was to face and make sense of them. With considerable reading, ACoA (Adult Children of Alcoholics) meetings and some helpful psychotherapy, I came to accept, understand, and manage painful feelings from my past.

"Among several issues, I learned to mourn the absence of my loving and alcoholic father, which included anger toward him and surprisingly toward my mother. My inner child blamed my mother as much as my father, albeit for different reasons. I guess I expected more from her. I came to realize that I was not really validated as a person of worth. It was like I was just there, not abandoned but not quite belonging either. I have accepted and mourned these past experiences that were painfully present, and I am healing. Now, I feel that there is a place for me, that I belong, that I am wanted. I feel more at peace with others and myself."

Keep in mind that the preceding questions and commentaries are for your benefit. Their purpose is to help you recognize and accept alcoholism that may exist in yourself and/or others. Without acceptance, living fails to improve; with acceptance, better living for self and others will occur.

7 Helping Normal Alcoholics

To reaffirm: The way we help and/or hinder alcoholics (oneself or others) highly depends on the way we construe alcoholism. For instance, we saw how an A.A. understanding of alcoholism engenders a treatment approach that differs from (though is not contradictory to) psychological approaches. The purpose of this book has been to offer a model of normal alcoholism that will contribute to our personal and professional models and treatments of alcoholism.

A premise has been that treatment approaches that exclude the spiritual dimension are not as effective as those programs that are more wholistic, that is: those that integrate the physical, psychosocial, and spiritual dimensions. Although normal alcoholics may not initially resonate with traditional A.A. or addiction programs, such wholistic programs have been, are, and can be beneficial to normal alcoholics. This chapter offers a few heuristic guidelines for helping oneself and others.

Admitting

Although admitting to alcoholism is necessary for recovery, it is difficult to achieve, for alcoholism is easy to deny, rationalize, minimize — or, not admit. Since many people assume that alcoholics are overly dysfunctional or abnormal, normal alcohol-

119

ics are not easily diagnosed. Once again, the way we construe alcoholism highly influences the way we cope with alcoholics.

Furthermore, some health professionals may minimize or misdiagnose normal alcoholism. At work, most managers do not really care about one's personal habits unless it impedes productivity. Moreover, our society, particularly through the mass media, endorses and fosters normal alcoholism. And finally, like all other alcoholics, normal alcoholics seldom accept their disorder.

Listen to this recovering alcoholic speak about confronting his actively normal alcoholic friend. "When I got actively involved in recovery, my friendship with Jack began to change. At one of our infrequent luncheons, Jack asked me if I thought he was an alcoholic. I told him that I didn't want to judge, but that I felt that he could be alcoholic. He said that he felt he had a drinking problem but he wasn't an alcoholic. He said he felt justified in drinking because it was one of the few pleasures he had in life and that he could do well with drinking. I didn't argue the point. I simply said I experienced alcohol differently. One of my points was only that life was better without drinking, not so much that life was bad with drinking.

"The sad thing for me is that our friendship changed. We are still friends, but our friendship is in transition. I don't know where it is going; hopefully it will get better, but it may just end. Although Jack and I were always close and still are, we now stand on different ground, and we both know it. We can still be close when we need to be but our viewpoints on drinking and enjoying life differ. Whether this difference will continue to get in the way, I don't know. I wonder if our friendship can grow or even maintain itself with Jack drinking and me not. It just seems that drinking and non-drinking don't mix very well."

Since acceptance is the gateway to recovery and nonacceptance maintains and fosters alcoholism, the first step toward sobriety is to increase the likelihood of breaking through nonacceptance to acceptance. Paradoxically, the way to acceptance is usually through nonacceptance. Alcoholics, with rare exceptions, must experience the painful consequence of drinking that is maintained and fostered by various forms of nonacceptance.

One popular model states that drinking and concurrent nonacceptance may lead alcoholics to hit "bottom" — a time and a place when and where they experience enough discomfort to motivate them to begin recovery. "Bottoming out" means that the pain of alcoholic drinking is experienced as more than the pain of becoming sober. Such alcoholics feel their powerlessness and begin to admit and recover from their alcoholism.

Most alcoholics in rehabs and in A.A. have "low bottoms," which often include serious personal, physical, professional, financial, legal, social, and religious difficulties. It seems that once alcohol enters their systems, they are virtually unable to manage appropriately. Unlike these alcoholics, many normal alcoholics seldom seem to hit bottom or if they do, they quickly bounce back to function fairly normally. Since they are able to function normally in spite of some of these negative consequences and therefore do not bottom out, they are unlikely to stop drinking. They seldom undergo problems to a severe degree. In short, the discomfort of normal alcoholism is unlikely to pressure them to recover.

To compound matters, some alcoholics admit intellectually to being alcoholic without fully realizing the gravity of their condition. Some reluctantly give rational assent to a "drinking problem" or to "possible alcoholism," but they fail to truly accept or surrender to being alcoholic. Metaphorically, they admit from their necks up, but do not accept in their guts and hearts. Although such ambivalence moves toward acceptance, it is usually not good enough to begin recovery.

June describes such ambivalence. "For years I knew I had a drinking problem, and I half-heartedly admitted to being an alcoholic. But, I got away with my drinking. No one, except my mother, complained. My friends, relatives, and Dad didn't seem to mind; the only thing they didn't like was my being single.

"Anyhow, I stayed out of trouble, did quite well in my law

practice, and stayed active in community and church affairs. I felt as happy or happier than most, and drinking seemed to be part of my well-being. So, although I knew I depended too much and too often on alcohol for comfort, I still got by quite nicely. Why quit? Only God knows why I did. But that's another story."

Co-alcoholics or co-dependents — those people who are enmeshed with and enable alcoholics — are also less likely to accept normal alcoholism. Despite feeling the effects of their loved one's drinking, they tend to focus on their functional success and deny the alcoholic drinking. Likewise, people in the work world and community are unlikely to diagnose alcoholic drinking as long as the alcoholic functions well. Keep in mind that our culture places high and perhaps paramount priority on functionality. The public rarely sees, let alone cares, about private consequences of alcoholism.

Furthermore, normal intervention strategies may not be very effective, for they depend on pointing out concrete examples of disruptive alcoholic behavior. Normal alcoholics usually avoid public disorder and keep private consequences secret. Nevertheless, intervention — to confront compassionately and concretely the alcoholic's behavior — is possible.

A group of people who know and care about the alcoholic can point out how their loved one's drinking pattern has harmed their lives. For instance, they can illustrate what it is like when he or she manipulates, isolates, or is unreliable. Such feedback must be given with compassion, acceptance, and loving detachment, while abstaining from critical analysis and judgment. Intervention does not guarantee that alcoholics will accept their disorder, but intervention does mean that family members and friends move away from their own enabling nonacceptance and toward acceptance. Consequently, co-addictive enabling is lessened, the dance of alcoholism moves differently, and therapeutic pressure is on the alcoholic.

Enabling and Detachment

Enabling is perhaps the most well-intentioned obstacle to acceptance and recovery. Enabling often centers around denying or rationalizing alcoholic behavior, taking responsibility for the alcoholic, and facilitating the alcoholic's drinking. Other examples of enabling include giving alcohol to alcoholics, excusing them from work, and rationalizing their alcoholic drinking. And, it is equally counterproductive to criticize, blame, shame, and try to control or stop alcoholics from drinking. To hide alcohol, to argue, to try to make the other feel guilty for drinking are also forms of enabling. Enabling usually means trying to be responsible for the alcoholic and consequently trying to control what we cannot control, namely: the alcoholic.

Detachment with love is usually necessary because of our co-dependent enmeshment with the alcoholic. Such enmeshment means that our well-being primarily depends on how the alcoholic acts, thinks, feels, and judges. Thus, when the alcoholic is happy, content, responsible, up, or unhappy, discontent, irresponsible, or "down," we feel basically the same way. Such attachment automatically leads to and fosters enabling, i.e., our involvement facilitates and nourishes the very behavior that we abhor. Paradoxically, it seems that the more we do for the alcoholic, the worse life gets.

Detachment means that we no longer "allow" the alcoholic to impact us so negatively. Rather than absorbing or taking too personally what the alcoholic does, we accept and let the addict be. Rather than arguing, being sarcastic, or blaming, we respect the alcoholic (not the behavior) and listen. Rather than enabling the addict, we let him or her experience the pain of his or her consequences. Rather than manipulating and being passive aggressive, (cold silence, manipulative speech, guilt games, martyr tears), we give concise and caring feedback. Rather than trying to control and cure, we give the alcoholic the opportunity to change.

Detachment also means that satisfaction of our needs and affirmation of our values do not depend on the alcoholic. Instead, we take care of our own needs and values rather than burdening the alcoholic with our welfare. We give up our willfulness and focus on what we can change — ourselves.

This mission is not easy, for we must detach with love. To detach indefinitely with indifference is worse than hate. Our goal is to detach from alcoholic processes (behavior, thinking, and feelings), and to love the person — self and/or other. To help alcoholics (or any addicts), we learn to detach from the alcoholic self and behavior, and to love the hidden person who is struggling to be free from alcohol and free for sobriety. To see with compassion the masked shame, guilt, fear, and panic is love. To love alcoholics without enabling, to let them suffer, to abstain from interfering, and yet to touch them with compassionate love are measures of very difficult love.

Rather than engaging in arguments, simply give clear, compassionate, and sufficient feedback. When the alcoholic denies such feedback, do not argue but simply state that this is what you perceive. For instance, you can say that you enjoy the alcoholic better when he is sober, and if asked, state how and why. Such feedback lets alcoholics reflect on their pattern of drinking and does not enable them to argue or divert the conversation. It is imperative neither to avoid nor try to change the alcoholic or his behavior, but instead accept the alcoholic and detach from the behavior.

To convey that you love the alcoholic regardless of his behavior is therapeutic, but his behavior is also important. For instance, you can tell him (preferably when he is dry) that you get upset because you love him and cannot get close to him when he is drinking. Or you can say that you feel uneasy when he is undependable and inconsistent, and when sober, you feel safer, more relaxed, and closer to him.

We have seen that persistent criticism, arguments, and/or blaming only reinforce alcoholic drinking. The more you do, the worse things get. And passive nonacceptance such as denial and avoidance only enables and may encourage the alcoholic to drink. Listen to Todd, who explains his wife's well-intentioned enabling. "As long as my wife was bitching about my drinking, I was in control. I was quick to point out that very few people made as much money as I did and that I was progressing in the firm. How could I be an alcoholic and be so successful, I reasoned.

"Furthermore, I would minimize my wife's demand that I be more reliable, dependable, and intimate with her. I would tell her that I was happy and question what was wrong with her. Soon, she would doubt herself, often feel guilty, and sometimes become angry and/or depressed. It was easy to manipulate her especially when she argued. I would simply focus on my success and divert her attention away from my deficits. And to prove I had no problem with intimacy, I would have sex with her. However, I shared little; ironically, sex was a way of hiding.

"My wife's constant criticism gave me an excuse to drink. I would rationalize that I had to cope with such stress, and in some ways this was true. Of course, I have learned that my drinking was an ineffective way of dealing with stress.

"Only when my wife stopped criticizing and accepted me as an alcoholic did I begin to feel pressured. Initially, I would try to argue with her, but she would not argue. The most she would say was that she felt drinking impeded our marriage and our well-being. Ironically, her allowing me to drink pressured me more than her trying to stop me. She let me have the consequences of my drinking, pointed them out, and then refused to argue the point. She stopped trying to change me. She would simply say this is what she experiences, and then let it go at that. No longer did her well-being depend on my sobriety.

"An effect of this new approach is that I could no longer divert the attention from my drinking onto her. Her refusal to try to change me put more pressure on me to listen to, look at, and change myself. No longer could I bitch about her bitching. No longer could I argue, but I had to listen to myself. It seemed that she was going on with life, and I was stuck. And yet, I knew that she loved me, but no longer did she depend on me the way she once did. Her compassionate detachment put more pressure on me than her previous attempts to control and change me. Paradoxically, the less she needed me to change, the more I needed to change."

On the other end of the gamut of nonacceptance are denial, avoidance, and minimization. Instead of doing too much, we try to do nothing. Rather than be over-involved, we are under-involved. Listen to this story. "Nobody in my family, husband, kids, mother and father, brothers and sisters, would ever think that I was an alcoholic. Not only did I take care of the house and people in it, but I also had a part-time job. In public I didn't drink much or often; all my drinking was done in private at night. And my workaholic husband went to bed about ten o'clock and really didn't see much of my drinking. Nobody seemed to mind.

"My drinking began to progress when I drank or started to drink in the afternoons and weekends. Nevertheless, I never drank so much that I could not take care of my responsibilities. I took care of them alcoholically, but no one knew the difference or seemed to care. However, a neighbor who lived with an alcoholic husband and a member of Al-Anon was the person who broke through my collusive denial. Finally a gentle voice shattered the silence.

"One afternoon she pointed out to me that she was concerned about my drinking. I explained that I had no idea what she was talking about, that I only drank to take the edge off of things, and that I functioned quite well. She did agree with me that I did function well, but that I frequently drank too much. She also pointed out that when I abstained from drinking, I was a different person. For some time my neighbor was a lone voice, and my husband and others thought she was a fanatic. Nevertheless, my neighbor's concern and words gnawed at my conscience.

"Well, I tried to prove to myself that I was not an alcoholic and to prove to my neighbor that she was wrong. I tried to stop for several months, but I had to admit that I had a great deal of difficulty not drinking. Eventually, I asked my neighbor what I could do to remain consistently dry. She encouraged me to go to A.A. and to hang in at the meetings. I hung in there and got sober."

Becoming Sober

We have proposed that the consequences of relatively dysfunctional alcoholism are more blatant and destructive than those of more functional alcoholism. And although alcoholics often progress in their drinking to become less functional, some maintain themselves for decades. Yet, these more normal alcoholics manifest negative behavior especially in their interpersonal and personal lives.

Some alcoholics stop drinking late in life, like in their fifties or sixties, but they do not become sober. Their abstinence is done out of will-power, not out of working a recovery program. In fact, many people who live with dry but less than sober alcoholics will say that in many respects these alcoholics are worse than when they were drinking.

Listen to Sue. "When Jim stopped drinking at the ripe old age of sixty-six, I thought life would be much better. But now he is withdrawn, grumpy, and overall a pain in the neck to live with. At least in his drinking days he was funny. It was no picnic living with him, but he was faithful, economically responsible, and good willed. But since he stopped drinking, he is worse than ever; sometimes I wish he would start drinking again."

The will-power or "white knuckle" approach to being sober seldom works. Although alcoholics can be dry for temporary periods of time or even permanently, they do not necessarily achieve sobriety. Sobriety means facing yourself, restructuring your life, and becoming a better person. Sobriety means that you experience a sense of inner serenity and improve your life personally and interpersonally. Sobriety includes and goes beyond functionality and manageability; it incorporates the spiritual life.

To achieve a healthier way of living, alcoholics must restructure their way of living in ways that foster wholistic growth. Mere abstinence without sobriety only results in so-called dry drunks or the same kind of alcoholic behavior, or worse. Recovery cannot be self-contained, but must incorporate realities greater than one's individual self. To go beyond oneself automatically combats alcoholic narcissism as well as giving nourishment and encouragement to progress.

It is not easy to change. Actually the only reality that is ultimately more difficult than change is trying not to change. To recover, alcoholics must learn to accept and manage short term discomfort in order to attain long term gains. To give up drinking and to achieve sobriety, alcoholics must accept the necessary discontent that initially comes from not drinking.

Simply to stop drinking leaves an enormous void — a gnawing emptiness that demands to be fulfilled. Consequently, dry alcoholics often replace their alcoholism with other addictions, like workaholism, overeating, sex, and religion. Others may simply isolate themselves and withdraw into books, television, or hobbies. None of these kinds of replacements foster sobriety, and sometimes they are worse than the alcoholism. Indeed, people cannot be perfect or free from all imperfections or even addictive tendencies. Our nature is to want to strive for perfection — for complete harmony, fulfillment, happiness — for heaven. So it is understandable that alcoholics are at least tempted to practice another addiction.

To recover, alcoholics must be able and willing to give up the sense in drinking — to accept that they will no longer have the dependable contentment, comforting buzz, or exciting license that they once experienced from drinking. Instead, they are challenged to find ways to replace alcoholic sense with better sense.

Most alcoholics also have to work through underlying feelings and thoughts that surface during sobriety. Instead of these feelings and thoughts being alcoholized, now they demand to be heard. Sometimes alcoholics go through turbulent times when they are dry and sober — times that are even more miserable than the hangovers they once experienced. Dependent or gamma alcoholics are often heard to say that their worst day sober is always better than their best day drinking. However, this is not always the case for all alcoholics. Some alcoholics feel and function better when drinking than in their early stages of recovery. Alcoholics can come to the time when they not only function better but overall are happier and healthier people without alcohol.

A pragmatic question is: What works best? What experiences foster healthiness — basic satisfaction, effective management, freedom, interpersonal intimacy, serenity, integrity, virtue. Addictions simply do not work well. Hence, alcoholics (actually anyone) must develop a program — a way of living — that fosters health. For many, Alcoholics Anonymous offers such a program.

My bias is to recommend to all alcoholics — from the most to the least functional — to try to practice a twelve step A.A. program for at least two years. Although many meetings may seem to be oriented toward more dysfunctional alcoholics, the twelve steps are just as valid and helpful to so-called functional or normal alcoholics. And there are often more normal (less dysfunctional) alcoholics than may initially meet one's eye. Remember: Only a dead alcoholic is completely dysfunctional.

A twelve step program is simply a good way of living, for it fosters wholistic living, openness and sharing, acceptance and reconciliation, healthy adjustment and contentment, and responsibility and accountability. To practice a twelve step program on one's own seldom works because without others it is too easy to regress and isolate oneself. To join in the fellowship of A.A. (regardless of the type of alcoholic you may be) is usually healing and life giving.

The A.A. twelve steps are actually ways to foster love's power and care for and from God, others, and self. Thus, it is primarily a spiritual program. The steps of A.A. focus on letting go of delusional willfulness, surrendering to God's healing love, reconciling with self and others, and helping oneself by helping others. Or as a recovering alcoholic summarized the steps: the first three steps deal with trusting God, and the next eight steps with cleaning your house, and the last step with helping others — or, with love and service.

Normal alcoholics can give A.A. a chance even though they may not initially feel at home or are suffering from a "terminal case of uniqueness." If they do not go to A.A., they must practice another program that encourages a consistent and structured way of healthy living. Like A.A., the program must be communal and structured, as well as offer interpersonal acceptance and encouragement, opportunities to communicate and manage, and ways to foster transcendent living.

In short, alcoholics of any type, must not only stay dry but also and more importantly grow in sobriety and health. Such recovery is not so much a goal to achieve but more of a perpetual process to experience. This life-project necessitates restructuring one's life in ways that consistently foster wholistic growth. Whether a "program" includes A.A., psychology, religion, philosophy, a social movement, a self-improvement group, or whatever or combination thereof, alcoholics have to think, feel, choose, act, live differently. Though recovery is not easy, any other way is more difficult — and, sobriety does become easier and pays off in priceless dividends.

8 Consequences of Sobriety

Our stories and analyses have contrasted alcoholic and sober living, proposing sobriety as a better way to live. Our message is not that alcoholics are bad or inferior people, but rather that alcoholics can become better. Although alcoholics pay a painful price for drinking, they can recover and enjoy the fruits of sobriety. Reflect on some of these consequences.

Serenity

Perhaps the most reliable, valid, and clearest symptom of sobriety is serenity. In fact, many recovering people use their serenity as a barometer to measure their sobriety. When they feel serene without addiction, they are probably sober. To be sure, serenity does not mean that everything and everyone are working in harmony, but rather within the core of our being resides a peace that persists regardless of environmental conditions.

Serenity is never perpetually perfect, although we may experience moments of perfection. Perfect and perpetual serenity is heaven. Rather, we grow in serenity, which means there are always some restive and restless feelings that challenge our serenity. Paradoxically, accepting the non-serene times enables us to strengthen our serenity. In fact, destructive forces challenge us and help us to be vigilant, never taking sobriety and serenity for granted. Serenity is partially born out of and nourished by possible chaos.

Such a paradoxical path to serenity is described by this Al-Anon member. "Every time my husband would push my buttons — I made a special effort to love myself. I saw these stressful times as opportunities to strengthen my detachment and acceptance, and to admit what I cannot change. Indeed, my serenity did not come as easily as it did when Bernie and I were in agreement, but it did come, and in many ways means more to me. Gaining serenity in the trying times gave me confidence, freedom, and self-esteem. Without these trying times, I don't think I would have grown as much. In a certain sense, I am grateful for my husband's alcoholism and for my co-dependency, for through them I have become a better me."

Serenity in stressful times is expressed in this way. "When my demons of drinking tempt me, I eye-ball them and tell them to return to their prior residence — to hell! Even though I can get upset with others or more often with myself, there is still an inner core of serenity that I know that I can bank on. It's sort of like I can be in the eye of a storm. There is always a place where I can see clearly, make sober decisions, and act sanely. God, what a feeling to know that true and lasting peace on earth is possible without drinking!"

Recovering alcoholics learn to avoid being seduced by alcoholism's false promises of fulfillment. Becoming free from willfulness (depending too much on oneself) and willessness (depending too much on others) as well as acquiring a healthy will (working with God and other wills) generates serenity. These serene recovering alcoholics no longer invest happiness in alcohol but in a sober self, sane others, and a helpful loving God.

However, we have seen that alcoholics want to be in heaven and are unwilling and/or unable to get there via the path of earth. They travel a road of self-deception that is strewn with counterfeits of serenity. Alcoholics believe a lie — that they can achieve sobriety merely with personal willpower and intelligence. Authentic serenity does not come from the temporary satisfactions of alcohol nor from individualistic efforts but rather from healthy relationships with God, others, and self.

Serenity often means that we accept what we cannot change and learn to live with it. Through loving detachment and other coping aids, we learn to live with what we dislike or hate. And, to be sure, sobriety and sanity do not purge the injustices, bad happenings, illnesses, cruelties, and crises of living, but we can cope in serenity.

An adult child of alcoholic parents expresses her serenity in this way. "For years I did things to achieve peace. I married an alcoholic man; I worked in a rehab center; I pressured my parents to make amends to me; I became a child advocate; I served on the school board, I gave talks on self-esteem. Although many of these activities were good, my hidden motivation included changing my painful past. I falsely assumed that if I could change realities in the present, my past would also change. So, I kept on repeating the same behavior expecting that some day the results would be different, namely, that I'd feel better inside myself. Finally, after working a program for some time, I came to accept my personal baggage. Instead of trying to get rid of the junk in my closet, I learned to live with it. You know what? When I obsessively tried to get rid of my junk, I was miserable. Since I have come to accept it, I experienced for the first time true serenity. Now, I love my whole self."

Serenity not only points to inner peace, tranquility, and harmony but also to clarity of vision, relaxed discipline, fluidity of thought, quiet strength, and decisive thinking. Serenity helps us to think clearly and to choose wisely. Without alcohol's disruptive forces, cognitive and volitional powers are strengthened, made freer, and become more effective. Becoming free from addictive thinking, self-pity, dishonesty, and egoism, we are freer to think clearly and act decisively. Because sober people are no longer entangled in the webs of alcoholism, their energies are released for effective thinking. No thing or no one can upset them as in the past so that their own thinking, feelings, and behavior stay on an even keel. Rather than trying to jump in stormy areas, they swim in the sea of serenity. Like a serene sea, we can experience depth, gentleness, refreshment, strength, and comfort.

Virtues

Along with serenity, other virtues are promised. In a real and practical way, recovering alcoholics can become virtuous persons — people of spirit. Becoming healthier and holier strengthens and frees them as well as appeals to and helps others. Reflect on some of these virtues.

Consider *faith* as a creative acceptance of experiences that go beyond rational explanation in spite of our doubts. In faith we gratuitously experience a reality that goes beyond and includes our rational faculties. This trans-rational experience broadens our vision, offers more possibilities and freedom, and strengthens us to make and implement healthy choices. Faith is not an abstract and passive substitute for coping, it is not a matter of: "If you do not experience it, have faith." On the contrary, faith is a concrete and creative approach involving an experience of a Higher Power that/who gives practical help.

Faith starves obsessive and scrupulous doubts that spring out of willfulness and perfectionism. In faith, we respond to a transcendent message that proclaims our ultimate helplessness and dependency on a higher and more powerful reality than ourselves. These words tell us that we need not be perfect to be okay or to be saved, that it is healthy to be imperfect and to need to be saved by another, that help is available from a Higher Power/Care — from others and God. Faith consumes unhealthy doubt with the fire of divine dependency.

Belief, which is more of a rational decision to follow certain truths, often precedes faith. We believe and practice what

others advise because we trust their judgment. And not infrequently, we believe in spite of and contrary to what we think and
feel. For example, we may have to believe in and therefore depend on a Higher Power because we see how such a practice has
been helpful to others. In a sense, we have to fake it in order to
make it. In time, our cognitive ascent can progress to faith so we
can experience a Higher Power/Care/God.

These are questions, however, that pressure us to look at
ourselves and that never let us be completely content. Doubt can
help us to take a personal inventory and to make amends as well
as reflect on our motives and behavior. And faith can enable us
to be open to our healthy self-questioning, to reflect on ourselves,
and to change what we can. Creative doubt actually challenges
and fosters faith, and faith embraces and facilitates questioning.

When we approach life only emotionally and/or rationally,
faith eludes us. To experience a transcendent reality, we have to
detach from our needs and thoughts. Experiencing a God who
cares makes practical sense. Faith helps us to accept reality, to
cope effectively, and to reside in serenity. Faith is particularly
helpful in achieving and fostering true recovery.

This recovering alcoholic shares a bit of his journey toward
faith. "One of my biggest obstacles to sobriety was my obsessive
intellectualizing; I had to have a reason for every feeling, thought,
and action. I felt compelled to analyze my motives and dynamics as well as those of others. When I spoke, I sounded like I was
giving scholarly lectures. Nothing was simple; everything was
complex. KISS — Keep it Simple and Spiritual — was especially
relevant to me. Of course, my intellectual and analytical approach
was a way to maintain control and to deceive myself.

"I had to accept that I didn't have to make rational sense
out of everything. I had to force myself to believe in the advice
of sober people, to stop thinking so much, be mentally silent, and
surrender to the realities that went far beyond my rational grasp.
Now, thank God, I can surrender to the mystery of life rather
than abuse it. Now I am enjoying life that is more than and yet a

part of me. My faith has not only saved me but also has opened up a new world to me."

Hope points out to an enduring vision of infinite possibilities in spite of our helplessness. In the first two years and prenatally, hope gets it's foundation from and emerges from basic trust in life — that life will, sooner or later, work out for the better in spite of our problems. It is as if hopeful people stand upright so that they can see beyond the immediacy of their stagnant situation to a life of choices that leads to effective and serene living. It is as if hopeless people lie paralyzed on their backs so that they fixate on the same realities. For instance, the vision of alcoholics without hope is narrow and constrained so that there are few possibilities and choices for change. Such alcoholics do not or are unable to trust God who can help liberate them; instead, they fight a losing and painful battle, becoming progressively trapped in their misery. Hopeful alcoholics do not give up; somehow they keep on moving in their recovery.

Paradoxically, hope is born out of helplessness. Feeling trapped or in despair, alcoholics (as well as co-alcoholics) can leap beyond their rational powers to a transcendent Power that helps them see light in the midst of darkness, to choose, to know that life can get better. Hope energizes and enables them to reach out to improve their lives.

Love is a paramount virtue without which life is meaningless. To love is to choose to act in ways that foster the welfare of others in the community in spite of our potential to violate ourselves and one another. Love for and from self, others, and God becomes the central motivating force of life. Indeed, love in and of itself is not enough, for we must learn to put our love into practice — to satisfy needs and achieve goals in ways that are congruent with love.

Recovering alcoholics come to healthy love. Alcoholics can stop their love affair with alcohol, come out of their isolation, and take the risk of loving people. They learn to do good for others without manipulation, to make amends and seek reconciliation, and to follow God's way. And, co-alcoholics realize that no matter how much they love, they cannot make the alcoholic sober and happy.

Perhaps even more difficult for alcoholics is learning to be loved and to love themselves. Letting ourselves be loved can be more risky than loving others because we allow ourselves to be seen and touched. Love from others and self-love melts the protective and suffocating prison of shame, breaks down the walls of isolation, and affirms and nourishes our worth. Rather than pursuing counterfeits of love, recovering alcoholics learn authentic love and its consequent strengths, joys, and healing.

Love for and from God as we understand God becomes paramount. Recovering people humbly connect with a reality that is greater than their individual self. They give up their self-will and tap into a transcendent will. Experiencing God's gift of love (grace), they give their life and will over to the care of God. Such surrender makes all the difference in the world. Alcoholics come to experience authentic strength and joy when living, working, and playing with God. It is an ecstatic relief to know experientially that they no longer have to save themselves. Recovering alcoholics pray for God's help, and God gives it to them.

Although most recovering alcoholics come to experience a God who cares for, helps, and provides for them, it is not necessary to construe the transcendent reality as a personal God. Agnostics, atheists, rationalists, non-believers, many Easterners, and others may not believe in such a personal God — and they need not do so to be helped. However, it is necessary to work with a reality that is more than one's individual ego. And love is the paramount way to be and go beyond oneself.

Perfect love does not exist on earth, nor is it for perfect people. Love is for imperfect, fallen, and broken people. We need love because we are on earth where demonic or negative forces exist. (In heaven, we will live perpetually in love — in serene harmony with self, others, and God.) Rather than deluding themselves with the heavenly high of alcohol, recovering people take the challenge to build a healthy community — to come closer to real heaven on earth.

Compassion, a hallmark of a healthy and maturing adult, etymologically means to suffer with another in love. In compassion, we help others to bear with the throes of living, and in our context the hardships of alcoholism. We recognize and appreciate that all of us, whether alcoholics/co-alcoholics or not, are pilgrims on a journey that includes many deserts and promised lands. Compassion is understanding and helping one another bear with pain in spite of life's inevitable burdens.

We are compassionate when we help alcoholics (or anyone) bear with the pain of their disorder. With detached love, we enter their world to see reality as they do, and we invite them to share their shame, guilt, fear, and helplessness. Appreciating their struggles lightens their burden and helps them to feel that they are not alone. And to know that someone is with and for you evokes hope, energy, and a sense of self-worth.

When alcoholics feel trapped, burned-out, guilty, resentful, or ashamed, compassion lifts them out of their dark pit and helps them to see new possibilities. They feel less burdened and lighter. Finally, someone knows how they feel.

To experience a person's being with and for you without judgment and with care is an enormously uplifting experience. You no longer feel like an alien or a senseless person but rather an integral and meaningful member of an understanding and supportive community. Getting out of the quagmire of isolation, alcoholics come to accept their limitations and affirm their unlimited worth from which healthy choices begin to emerge.

Compassionate persons are like loving warriors. On one hand, they are truly concerned with and care for others. Their love for others strives to be without conditions, seeking to do what helps others simply and basically because they are who they are. On the other hand, compassionate people are also warriors. They have faced and fought many battles, have been wounded, admitted and cared for their weakness, and have become strong.

Enemies, pain, evil, danger, injustice, and shame are not foreign to them, for they have traveled these and other valleys of darkness. Paradoxically, they feel at home with such demons and can help people accept and manage them with strength and integrity rather than shying away and intellectualizing them. With strong and gentle love, they journey with them through their deserts that eventually lead to promised lands of dignity and freedom.

Not only does sobriety include and evoke compassion for others but also compassion for oneself. When alcoholics stand strong in love for themselves, their burdens are lightened and they are liberated from self-destructive coping and freed for healthy choices. Being compassionate with themselves lifts the veil of shame and rekindles and nourishes their worth. For instance, to be compassionate with the wounded child within is especially important for healing and recovery.

For many recovering alcoholics accepting that they need help from a Higher Power evokes the compassion of a personal God. They experience a Divine Care that helps them carry the burdens of their ongoing recovery. Their God is not someone who takes away their struggles or who makes everything all right, nor is God seen as the opium of the masses. But rather God helps them to cope, offers courage, encourages choice, and laughs and cries with them. God struggles with them to heal in a broken world — and, often without our knowing, God carries them along the way.

We also grow in patience and fortitude. *Patience* is waiting in love for the right time in spite of willfulness and willessness. Rather than acting too quickly or impulsively, sober people learn to take their time to reflect and make sensible decisions. They learn to allow life, themselves, and others to emerge in due time. Rather than trying to make things happen or to force change before its time, they wait for the right time. Sometimes inaction is faster and better than action.

Perfectionists have difficulty in letting people achieve their goals according to their time and ways. Feeling they know what is the right way, they project their own standards and time schedule on others. Perfectionists have trouble letting people be, let alone letting them grow according to their calling. Patience ameliorates their need to control and reminds them that all people have their time. A Turkish proverb reminds us that "patience is the key to paradise."

Pilgrim people come to realize that there is a time (*Kairos*) for all seasons — a time to fast and a time to feast, a time to laugh and a time to cry, a time to run and a time to rest, a time to speak and a time to be silent, a time to interact and a time to be alone, a time for conflict and a time for peace, a time to be lonely and a time to love, a time to be blind and a time to see, a time to be lost and a time to be found, a time to be foolish and a time to be wise, a time to change and a time to accept, a time to control and a time to surrender, a time for suffering and a time for joy, a time to die and a time to live.

Fortitude is also a virtue that progressively emerges from sober/healthy living. Fortitude means that we stand strong in love despite our weakness. Alcoholics grow in the courage (strength of heart) to say no to the seduction of an easy high. They grow progressively stronger in their sobriety which allows them to be more decisive and freer to enjoy life. Paradoxically, for many alcoholics fortitude emerges from accepting their powerlessness and surrendering to God. Admitting we are powerless empowers us.

Recovery/sobriety/health also results in the paradoxical unity of pride and humility. *Pride* is taking delight in being an integral member of God's community of humankind in spite of the possibility of feeling worthless and/or of being isolated. Rather than a false, neurotic pride that is rooted in perfectionism, recovering alcoholics experience healthy pride in following the paths of sobriety and goodness. Rather than tripping off into themselves via alcohol, alcoholics reach out to genuinely care for and connect with others. Rather than withdrawing, aggressing, or compulsively pleasing, they choose to live without manipulation. They depend on a Higher Care who serves as the sustaining source of their worth and who propels them toward building community. They can say "yes!" to life.

Yet, recovering alcoholics are *humble*; they know their place on earth — that as isolated individuals they are powerless over their disorder and ultimately over life. Humility is knowing the place on earth (*humus* = earth) that empowers us in spite of our arrogance. Rather than holding to a false humility of looking down, healthy people get down on their knees and look up to their Reason for Being. They humbly ask a Greater Care for help and with humble pride accept this unending care. As one recovering alcoholic said, "We learn to be both proud and humble — to be 'prumble.'"

These and other virtues grow with ongoing sobriety. As we have indicated, virtue is often built on and paradoxically motivated by its opposite vice. It is difficult to grow in faith, hope, love, compassion, patience, fortitude, pride, and humility without doubt, helplessness, violence, burdens, impulsiveness/compulsiveness, weakness, self-effacement, and self-aggrandizement. To be sure, a virtuous life progressively fosters recovery — our letting go, letting be, and letting grow.

Forgiveness

Although forgiveness is one of the most healing and desired consequences of sobriety, it is often misunderstood. Many people falsely assume that, as if by magic, forgiveness makes everything all right. This "old" notion meant that to confess and ask for forgiveness implied that all our faults were purged, forgotten, cleansed, "whitewashed" — or, that suddenly we were changed from sinner to saint. And, furthermore, the common but misleading saying "forgive and forget" often led to unnecessary difficulties. Although there is truth in this mechanical "cure all" approach, true forgiveness is much richer and more creative.

Consider another way of looking at forgiveness, namely, as accepting another unconditionally in love. True forgivers accept others as they are. They do not pretend that the past never happened, that all is well, that there will never be a wrong committed again. And neither do they harbor resentment and vindictiveness, holding grudges — all of them conditions contrary to love.

To forgive is to "give for" another. Good people do not forgive to make themselves feel good (though this is often a natural consequence), to patronize or control a person, or to "get a high place in heaven." They give to and for another's welfare (and therefore their own as well) without strings attached. To be embraced in love when you are at your best is indeed invigorating and affirming. But to be accepted and loved without interrogation, criticism, or patronization when you are at your worst is even more important. When you have done wrong, are sinful, embarrassed, shameful, dirty, ugly, naked, and vulnerable, and you are embraced with compassionate and unconditional love, you feel accepted, loved, consoled, reconciled, renewed, and healed.

Forgiveness leads to consolation and reconciliation. When forgiven, people feel whole, more one with themselves and others. Rather than feeling desolate (*de-solus* = very much alone), they feel consoled (*cum-solare* = very much comforted by others). Their integrity and dignity are restored, and in a sense they feel reborn. Being loved with their faults, not as perfect but as fallen persons, liberates them from feeling rejected or alienated, and they feel in harmony with others — once again more fully human and alive. Forgiven people are prodigal daughters and sons who are welcomed home and embraced by loving parents.

Forgiveness is also a "fore-giving." It is a loving acceptance that is always in readiness to be given. Like the father of the prodigal son, healthy and holy people wait in patience and hope for their loved ones to return home. Their healing love is ready to be given even "before" it is asked for. Once again, it is without any conditions — a love waiting to be given. Even when someone does not ask for forgiveness or refuses forgiveness, the one pardoning still offers it perpetually. No matter what, true forgivers are ready to welcome their loved ones back home.

To be sure, healthy people do not condone, minimize, or excuse immoral or destructive behavior. They reject evil acts and forgive (accept in love) the person. In fact, forgiveness allows and encourages the forgiven to admit, learn from, and make amends as much as possible. Rather than saying that everything is alright, people in recovery try to grow from and make restitution from their faults. Instead of forgetting, they freely *remember*.

To try to forget reinforces memories and exacerbates pain. To bear grudges, become passive aggressive, or play martyr roles all militate against forgiveness. Forgiving people remember because they know that demons (negative forces, faults, the potential for evil) seldom die — and, they remember to be vigilant to cope with the demons when they appear.

Not only can recovering people seek forgiveness from others but they can also forgive themselves. To embrace your whole self including your dark, ugly, and sinful side is difficult yet essential to recovery. Without self-forgiveness, recovering alcoholics are perpetually at odds with themselves. To continue recovery, they must accept and love their broken and wounded selves in order to heal, stand up, and move forward.

Instead of reprimanding, blaming, rejecting, or being indifferent, we are called to forgive our past imperfections and transgressions as well as those who transgressed against us. To forgive oneself, parents, and any other significant persons comes with recovery. To reconcile with the past dissipates pain and fosters healing.

There is also forgiveness from God who judges justly and even more so is merciful and loving. The love of a God is made for fallen people. Divine forgiveness, unlike human forgiveness (from others or self), is always available, never taken away, always extended, never conditional, always dependable. Whatever name you want to give this Transcendent Reality — God's Presence, our Spirit or Higher Power, Ultimate Concern, Divine Love, our Mother / Father — is always there for us, ready to touch our shameful and wounded self, to extend a hand to support us, to embrace us, to walk with us, to be with us no matter what. The help, hope, and healing of God's forgiveness is our saving grace and perhaps God's greatest gift to us.

Growing in Health

Acceptance of our fallenness, alcoholism, co-dependence or whatever disorder, initiates, maintains, and nourishes progressive and healthy growth. Recovery is not a state or condition of being dry and sober, but more a process of growing in sobriety, a challenging journey that never ends. We are pilgrim people always on the way of greater health.

Recovery brings physical consequences. People in recovery simply function, feel, and look better; in fact it is common to hear comments about how much better they look. Their physiology is invariably and significantly improved. Not only do they feel better but also they are stronger and less vulnerable to becoming ill. Physical activities are much easier and enjoyably, clothes fit better, work is more efficient and productive, more energy and time are experienced. Instead of violating themselves, recovering alcoholics take care of their physical selves. Indeed, it feels good to be alive.

Recovering alcoholics also manage their lives significantly better. Coming out of alcoholism, they can think more clearly and act decisively. Rather than being impulsive, irrational, narcissistic, self-willed, withdrawn, aggressive, or dependent, they manifest creative control, rational judgment, genuine care, assertiveness, gentle patience, and inter-dependence. Overall, they function much better than when they were addicted. They manage to work, cope, think, choose, interact, solve, compete, study, read, speak, look, listen, and learn better. Even more important than physical and psychosocial health is growth in the spiritual life.

Recovering people can come to know the meaning of Divine Providence. We have seen that it is useful to sense the presence of a Reality that is more than and greater than oneself, and cares and provides for us. Somehow and somewhere healthy people experience (not necessarily consciously) a reality that is inexplicably beyond their rational grasp, a mysterious yet intimate presence that they can depend on for guidance and counsel. This is not spiritual wish-fulfillment or double talk, but rather a clinical and effective phenomenon. Observe and listen to the many recovering people now and throughout the ages who have experienced and given witness to God granting them the serenity to accept what they could not change, courage to change what they could change, and the wisdom to know the difference.

As alcoholic (and co-alcoholic) people continue to journey on the road of recovery, they catch glimpses of a transcendent existence, hear silent music, step to the music that was created for them, taste a bit of the Divine, smell its heavenly aroma, feel what it is like to be for a time in heaven. No longer are they seduced by alcoholic counterfeits, but they opt to stoop low (accept their powerlessness) to experience a healthy and permanent high. They can actually rise from the dead (of alcoholism) to life.

Coming through the dark nights of alcoholism eventually and ultimately lead to never-ending days of light. In time, pilgrim people come to see the Promised Land and live forever in harmony with one another and God. Then, there will be no more dark and painful times, wounded bodies-minds-spirits, broken and fearful relationships, temporary loves, and sick and suffering communities. Then, there will be light and joyful times, healed bodies-minds-spirits, wholesome and open relationships, and the exhilaration of being perfectly and perpetually in love.

Selected Bibliography

Alcoholics Anonymous. New York: Alcoholics Anonymous World Services, Inc., 1976.

Alcoholics Anonymous Comes of Age. A Brief History of A.A. New York: Alcoholics Anonymous World Services, Inc., 1985.

Alcoholics Anonymous. Twelve Steps and Twelve Traditions. New York: Harper/Hazelden, 1987.

American Psychiatric Association: Diagnostic and Statistical Manual of Mental Disorders. Fourth edition, revised. Washington, DC: American Psychiatric Association, 1994.

Anderson, Daniel J. *Perspectives on Treatment.* Minnesota: Hazelden, 1981.

Baltimore, Carmella and John. *Teenage Alcoholism and Substance Abuse.* Florida: Frederick Fell Publishers, 1988.

Beattie, Melody. *Co-Dependent No More.* New York: Harper/Hazelden, 1987.

_____. *Beyond Co-Dependency and Getting Better All the Time.* New York: Harper/Hazelden, 1989.

Berg, Insookim and Scott D. Miller. *Working With the Problem Drinker.* New York: W.W. Norton and Company, 1992.

Blume, Sheila B. *The Disease Concept of Alcoholism Today.* Minnesota: Johnson Institute Books, 1983.

Co-Dependency. An Emerging Issue. Florida: Health Communications, Inc., 1984.

147

148 THE NORMAL ALCOHOLIC

Collins, Vincent C. *Acceptance*. Indiana: Abbey Press, 1979.

Coombs, Robert H. and Douglas M. Ziedonis. *Handbook on Drug Abuse Prevention. A Comprehensive Strategy to Prevent the Abuse of Alcohol and Other Drugs*. Boston: Allyn and Bacon, 1995.

Courage to Change. New York: Al-Anon Family Groups Headquarters, Inc., 1992.

Dorff, Frances. *The Art of Passingover*. New Jersey: Paulist Press, 1988.

Doweiko, Howard E. *Concepts of Chemical Dependency*. Belmont, CA: Brooks/Cole Publishing Co., 1990.

Ellis, Albert, et. al. *Rational Emotive Therapy with Alcohol and Substance Abusers*. New York: Pergammon Press, 1988.

Fichel, Ruth. *The Journey Within A Spiritual Path to Recovery*. Deerfield Beach, FL: Health Communications, Inc., 1987.

Hester, Reid K. and William R. Miller (Eds.). *Handbook of Alcoholism Treatment Approaches*. New York: Pergammon Press, 1989.

Hodgson, Harriet. *Parents Recover Too*. Minnesota: Hazelden, 1988.

How to Use Intervention in Your Practice. Minnesota: Johnson Institute Books, 1987.

Jellinek, E.M. *The Disease Concept of Alcoholism*. New York: Hillhouse Press, 1960.

Julia H. *Letting Go With Love. Help for Those Who Love an Alcohol/ Addict Whether Practicing or Recovering*. New York: St. Martin's Press, 1987.

Knott, David H. *Alcohol Problems*. New York: Pergammon Press, 1986.

Knowlton, Judith and Chaitin, Rebecca. *Detachment*. New Jersey: Perrin & Tragett, 1985.

Kraft, William F. *Whole and Holy Sexuality*. Indiana: Abbey Press, 1989.

_____. *Achieving Promises. A Spiritual Guide for the Transitions of Life*. Philadelphia: Westminster Press, 1981.

Kurtz, Ernest. *A.A.: The Story*. San Francisco: Harper and Row, 1988.

Larsen, Ernie. *Stage II: Recovery. Life Beyond Addiction*. New York: Harper/Hazelden, 1986.

Lerner, Harriet Goldhan. *The Dance of Intimacy*. New York: Perennial Library, 1989.

May, Gerald G. *Addiction and Grace*. San Francisco: Harper and Row, Publishers, 1989.

Nakken, Craig. *The Addictive Personality*. MN.: Hazelden, 1988.

Nemeck, Francis Kelly, OMI, and Coombs, Marie Theresa, Hermit. *O Blessed Night: Theological Underpinnings for Recovery from Addiction, Codependency and Attachment according to St. John of the Cross and Teilhard de Chardin*. New York: Alba House, 1991.

One Day at a Time in Al-Anon. New York: Al-Anon Family Groups Headquarters, Inc., 1987.

Robertson, Nan. *Getting Better Inside Alcoholics Anonymous*. New York: William Morrow & Co., Inc., 1988.

Silverstein, Lee M. *Consider the Change. The Choice is Yours*. Pompano Beach, FL: Health Communications, Inc., 1986.

Torok, Lou. *When You Hurt*. New York: Alba House, 1999.

The Twelve Steps. A Healing Journey. Minnesota: Hazelden Foundation, 1986.

The Twelve Steps of Alcoholics Anonymous. New York: Harper/Hazelden, 1987.

Twerski, Abraham. *Caution: "Kindness Can Be Dangerous to the Alcoholic."* New Jersey: Prentice Hall, 1981.

Wholey, Dennis. *The Courage to Change*. New York: Warner Books, Inc., 1984.

York, David & Phyllis. *Tough Love*. New York: Bantam Books, 1983.

Vogler, Roger E. and Wayne R. Barto. *The Better Way to Drink*. Oakland, CA: New Harbinger Publications, 1985.

Wuthnow, Robert. *Sharing and the Journey*. New York: The Free Press, 1994.

This book was designed and published by St. Pauls/Alba House, the publishing arm of the Society of St. Paul, an international religious congregation of priests and brothers dedicated to serving the Church through the communications media. For information regarding this and associated ministries of the Pauline Family of Congregations, write to the Vocation Director, Society of St. Paul, 7050 Pinehurst, Dearborn, Michigan 48126 or check our internet site, www.albahouse.org